ERICH SCH

TRAVELS

IN

INDIA AND KASHMIR

Volume 2

Elibron Classics
www.elibron.com

Elibron Classics series.

ISBN 1-4021-8918-4 (paperback)
ISBN 1-4212-9616-0 (hardcover)

This Elibron Classics Replica Edition is an unabridged facsimile of the edition published in 1853 by Hurst and Blackett, London.

Dewar Talaw.

London, Hurst and Blackett, 1853.

TRAVELS

IN

INDIA AND KASHMIR.

BY

THE BARON ERICH VON SCHONBERG.

IN TWO VOLUMES.

VOL. II.

LONDON:
HURST AND BLACKETT, PUBLISHERS,
SUCCESSORS TO HENRY COLBURN,
13, GREAT MARLBOROUGH STREET.
1853.

LONDON:
Printed by Schulze and Co., 13, Poland Street.

CONTENTS

OF

THE SECOND VOLUME.

CHAPTER I.

CHAPTER II.

CHAPTER III.

CHAPTER IV.

CHAPTER V.

CHAPTER VI.

CHAPTER VII.

CHAPTER VIII.

CHAPTER IX.

CHAPTER X.

CHAPTER XI.

CHAPTER XII.

CHAPTER XIII.

CHAPTER XIV.

CHAPTER XV.

CHAPTER XVI.

CHAPTER XVII.

TRAVELS

IN

INDIA AND KASHMIR.

CHAPTER I.

Kashmir—A Sirdar in coat of mail—Appearance of the city—Chahar Chenar—Audience with the governor—The lake—The floating gardens—Kashmerian boatmen—Attempts on my freedom—Difficulty in buying a horse—Bad news from Lahore—Murder of Scheer Singh—The Dhassera festival—Difficulties of my position at Kashmir—Apprehensions of an English invasion.

KASHMIR, the reputed cradle of the human race, that spot to which the sagas of the eastern nations have lent a religious veneration, and which the imaginings of the western poets have robed in all the beauties of an earthly Elysium —Kashmir, around which is flung all the voluptuousness of Asiatic fiction, and so much of the splendour of Asiatic history — where is the European who hears Kashmir mentioned, and does not think of the glory of Ackbar, the pomp of Jehanghir, and the beauty of Nur Jehan? Where is the European traveller, particularly the sentimental one, who, in turning his steps towards the East, has not thought of Kashmir? How many a restless spirit has thought that *there,* in the cradle of the human family, he might find a solution of the mystery that perplexed him when he considered his own being, or the various conditions of his race. But let him come to Kashmir, and what does he find? The sheltering mountain, the winding river, the unruffled lake, the floating gardens, and above all the balmy air, are even as he had pictured them; but all are filled with memories, or peopled with fancies. The ruins that lie about speak of man only as a being that had passed by the way, leaving no record whence he came or whither he was gone. His works speak of him as a conqueror, or a destroyer; the great problem is still unsolved, and the longing eye and the unsatisfied heart still strain after the unattainable. But are not these very longings and these disappointments an answer to our inquiries?

When within a short distance of Kashmir, I was met by a high sirdar, a general, whom Schaykh Gulam Muhyiddin sent to escort me. This sirdar was the first warrior I had seen, fully equipped in coat-of-mail, and I was surprised at his imposing appearance. His coat, or shirt of mail, was of chain armour, and reached to the knee. His round helmet was adorned with a plume of three heron feathers, his shield hung upon his back, and his trusty sabre by his side. A handsome, high-mettled horse was managed with perfect ease by this modern knight, whose fine person and prepossessing features tended not a little to show his warlike accoutrements to advantage. These suits of armour are much less general here now, than formerly; they are only to be found with rich persons, who keep an armourer in pay. Sometimes, but rarely, a suit may be offered for sale.

My munschi and Lala Mackermal, the functionary sent by the governor of Kashmir to attend me, accompanied me in the howdah. The sirdar with his horsemen formed an escort. My suite was now swelled to a considerable number. My personal attendants amounted to twenty-six: munschi, khidmatgar, wardrobe-keeper, cooks, washers, says, ferasche, &c. Then there was the mehmendar, or lieutenant with his troop of forty men, the munschi, Lala Mackermal and his attendant, the thanahdar, and his people; these, with the sirdar and his horsemen, and about seventy coolies and bearers, not to mention numbers that curiosity had attracted from the city, enabled me to make a very imposing entry into Kashmir.

The city of Kashmir, formerly called Serry-nagor, or the abode of the king, is one of the oldest oriental towns. It is less handsome, examined in detail, than when seen at a distance, as is generally the case with Asiatic cities. Another disadvantage as to beauty of appearance, is, that the rear of the houses is turned towards the street, and is generally enclosed with walls. The narrowness of the streets in oriental cities, and their filth and poverty-stricken appearance are proverbial, and this wretchedness of aspect is owing, in a great measure, to the caprice of the richer inhabitants, who do not wish to dwell near one another: on the contrary, they try to keep as far asunder as possible, so that the space between the houses of two rich men is often occupied by miserable hovels. Seen from a distance, all eastern towns present an attractive appearance, with their minarets, domes and mosques, their mausoleums and lovely gardens; but the traveller, deceived by this prospect so alluring in the distance, finds, on a nearer approach, beside the stately mosque and graceful minaret a heap of ruins, and of all that looks so attractive, the trees alone will bear a close view. The gardens are kept in good order, and afford a refreshing shade to all.

In Kashmir there are few minarets or domes: there are no mausoleums outside the town. The mosques and towers are built of wood, and in consequence, their form is different from that seen in other cities. The houses have rather an European appearance with their roofs of slate, or wood. It is no wonder that there are no mausoleums to be seen here, as the conviction that in a few years, the worm, or the damp mould would destroy the edifice, must naturally prevent the erection of such monuments. All the buildings of Kashmir are, on account of the material used in the erection, very paltry.

In looking down on Kashmir, that which most strikes the traveller, is the lake lying immediately behind the city, the river that winds through it, connected with the lake by a canal, the fort that lies upon the left bank of the river, and the governor's house upon the right. This dwelling is fortified. The fort is the abode of the military commander, and is provided with cannon, and many implements of war. It would not, however, in case of attack form a military position, but would be merely sufficient to resist the efforts of an undisciplined mob.

I have already remarked that in oriental towns, the houses of the rich are generally far asunder, but in Kashmir, along the banks of the river, this is not the case. The jealous householders have here no need to fear the prying eye of their opposite neighbour, and do not shun contact with his dwelling. These houses three and four stories high, are handsome, and well and regularly built, with flat, projecting roofs. The banks of the river present a charming appearance. Every house has a door and flight of steps conducting to the water, and here the boat or gondola is moored.

In the midst of the lake is the little island Chahar Chenar, on which is built a small kiosk, which though not handsome, has been the scene of many a royal revel, and here, when night flung her soft veil over the landscape, thousands of lamps peering from amid the leafy trees, gave to the whole isle the aspect of a fairy festival. A little to the right of Chahar Chenar at the foot of the mountain, is seen the shadowy outline of some fine trees, wrapt in the blue mist of distance. Here lies the Schalimar, the favourite retreat of Jehanghir, and built by him for his beloved Nur Jehan, with whom he generally passed the summer months in this delightful retreat. A short canal connects the lake with the garden, which is ornamented with well-planted terraces and beautiful fountains.

The house is very simple, containing only two chambers, and on either side is a large verandah. There are two small houses or wings, which contain several chambers. Behind the main building is a reservoir, and several beautiful fountains. The entire is surrounded with majestic trees.

At some distance outside the city, lie on a bare plain the ruins of two palaces. They are evidently of great antiquity, and though of a fine style of architecture, not so handsome as Jehanghir's palace, the Schalimar. About two hour's journey from the city, rises a mountain, the last of the ridge that encloses the lake on the east. It is called the Takht-i-Suliman, a title which has evidently been given by the Mahomedans, who, of course, suppressed the Sanscrit name. A Brahmin of my acquaintance, though a pretender to great learning, could not give me any information on the subject.

Nature offers many sources of enjoyment to the inhabitants of this lovely valley, but the stern spirit of the oppressor nips their pleasures. For myself I must say that from the time I put my foot in the valley, all was for me, mirth and harmony, sport and play. My evenings were crowned with song and dance; my table was spread with the choicest fruit, and adorned with the most odoriferous flowers. My thanadar did not fail to exercise to the full, the powers invested in him, knowing that his authority would be of short duration.

On the day of my arrival in Kashmir, a prodigious crowd accompanied me to the river-side, where a boat awaited to conduct me to the Schalimar, which had been appointed for my residence. Multitudes thronged by land and water to see me. I gave directions to my people to proceed to the river-side; but the pressure was so great, that we could scarcely advance a step. I bethought me of an expedient. I ordered money to be flung amongst the crowd. The mass divided, a space was left, we advanced; again the throng closed in, and again was the golden talisman applied to remedy the evil; and thus, it may be said, that I purchased my passage to the lake. But I was not yet free; boats filled with women crowded round me, for whose departure I was obliged to pay. The distance of the garden from the place of embarkation was three coss. The boat into which I entered was remarkably long, affording place for fifty rowers.

When I arrived at the Schalimar, I found myself in peace. The building in the garden is simple, but seemed to me to be firmly built. All around were beautiful fountains and noble plane trees, but I thought my dwelling a little too far from the city. The governor sent his compliments, and let me know that everything was arranged for an audience on the following morning. Accordingly, at an early hour the next day, the elephants arrived, and I set out to meet the governor. The palace in which he lives is, properly speaking, the only one in the valley of Kashmir; for I will not reckon as palaces the ruins that remain since the time of the emperors.

When I arrived at the palace, I found a great number of military drawn out. All seemed well disciplined, and wore handsome uniforms. When I reached the inner court, I alighted at the steps that led to the house; and here some of the high civil officers received me. I was then conducted into the chamber, in which the divan was assembled. Here the governor, or, as he is generally called, the Schaykh Sahab, received me, and conducted me to a seat on his right hand. The members of his family took their places next the governor, and after them, the high nobility. These were seated on silver moras, or footstools; next were the sirdars and high officers of the crown, seated on carpets. The hall of audience was divided by a partition of lattice-work into two parts, so that the part in which we sat formed a parallelogram, at the upper end of which the Schaykh Sahab and I sat; the long sides were occupied by the nobles, and the civil and military officers; and the end opposite to that where the governor and I sat, was occupied by the dancing-girls, who, upon such occasions, are always present to add variety to the scene, though there is little notice taken of them.

The Schaykh Sahab, Gulam Muyhiddin, expressed himself in the most friendly terms, and declared repeatedly that I had only to command, and that all should be done according to my wishes; that such were the orders of my royal friend Scheer Singh, which fully coincided with his own wishes to serve me. He said that everything was ready for my journey to Pyr Penjal, and requested me to visit the places in the neighbourhood of my residence, and see whether I should prefer any to that in which I was staying, telling me again that the orders of the maha-rajah were that everything should be placed at my disposal. After these complimentary speeches, a matchlock was brought, which had been manufactured in Kashmir, according to a model obtained from M. Jacquemont, and presented to me. I now, as is the custom, requested permission to retire; upon which the Schaykh Sahab anointed me with rose-oil, and I withdrew with the same ceremony with which I had entered. If the custom of taking off the shoes when stepping over a carpeted room is in some sense praiseworthy, it is very laughable, at the termination of large meetings like that I have been describing, to see the high functionaries running and pressing in the narrow passages that lead to Indian chambers, in search of their shoes. It is well for Europeans that they are exempted from this ceremony.

Upon the first day of my arrival, presents were brought to me in the name of the Maharajah, Scheer Singh. These consisted of the usual preserves, fruit, a purse of money, flowers, &c. On my return to my garden-home, after my audience with the governor, I received fresh presents—bürmusk, a delightful perfume, pickles and fruits, and money for my munschi and servants. In the evening dancing-girls arrived, and after them, several of the notables of the city paid me a visit.

On the following day, I made a tour of the lake, partly to become acquainted with the locality, and partly that I might visit those places which, I had been told, were at my disposal. As far as regarded a change of residence, I found that the Schalimar was far preferable to the castles in the neighbourhood, which were all in ruins; and though I had wished to come nearer to the city, I now resolved to remain where I was.

The lake is very handsome, the water fresh,

and abundantly supplied with fish, wild-duck, and water-fowl. No Kashmerian traveller has omitted to speak of the floating gardens. I should be more inclined to call them rafts, besprinkled with clay, pushed into the water, for the most part planted with melons and cucumbers, that seem to thrive very well. The poor boatmen of Kashmir, who constitute a large portion of the inhabitants, strive in this way to procure themselves a little garden, of which the produce escapes taxation as long as it it is not offered for sale, and this may be one of the causes of the encroachment on the lake, though the fruitfulness of the soil is undoubtedly another.

The boat is the house, the kitchen, the home of its master. In the morning he rows towards the city, sells the produce of his garden, and purchases what he may require: then rows his house here or there, as the sunshine or shade may invite. Thousands of people live here in this manner, and in Kashmir, as in Venice, almost all intercourse is carried on by water. The boats in which these people live are furnished with roofs of matting, a portion of the forepart is cut off for the use of the family, while the remainder is left open. The women understand the management of the oar, and it is they who generally row the boats to market.

I passed three weeks of tedious existence in the Schalimar, wearied with intrigues, the object of which seemed to be to make me a prisoner without using violence. There was at length no doubt that every means of leaving the Schalimar had been cut off, and that the extent of my rambles must now be confined to an excursion on the lake, or a promenade in the adjoining gardens. This proceeding was in the commencement inexplicable, but the accounts that soon afterwards reached me from Lahore solved the mystery. I was not allowed to want for anything, nor was I treated with less politeness than on my arrival; but my movements were in every way circumscribed. Boats arrived every day with provisions, fruits, and flowers for my use. Natsch girls were sent in the evening to amuse me and wile away the time; but every wish that I expressed to leave the Schalimar, or journey beyond its precincts, was refused—not indeed directly, but with a plausible excuse.

On the way from Lahore I had lost my horse, and had not since bought another. During the journey I had not cared to look for one, because I was told that in Kashmir I should find horses of every kind. Since my arrival in the Schalimar I had repeatedly ordered that horses should be sent for my inspection, but I was always told that it was impossible to find any. At length, not being able to restrain my impatience, I made some efforts to attain my object. Some horses were sent me, but such animals! there could have been no doubt that I would not buy them. I was very much annoyed, and after repeated expostulations a good horse was brought, and as the price was not extravagant I concluded the bargain. No sooner was this done than the owner mounted the horse, rode about for some time, and then disappeared. It was impossible for me to pursue him, for in showing off the paces of the horse he had remained upon one side of the canal while I was on the other. My disappointments had been so frequent that I could no longer doubt it was a contrivance of an enemy.

I had been ill, and was now become seriously unwell, a violent fever prostrating my strength. With the assistance of Heaven the goodness of my constitution triumphed; my strength gradually returned, and with it my impatience of the prison-life, that I became anxious to escape. My representations were met by evasive answers. I declared that my health would no longer permit me to remain in this abode, where I had caught fever; but my remonstrances were useless, though no open opposition was offered to me. The prime mover of all these intrigues was Lala Mackermal.

It happened that one day he did not come to me as usual; perhaps he was occupied in caballing somewhere else. It so chanced that on this day my munschi met an Affghan who had a horse to sell; the animal suited me, and I bought it.

Next morning, when Lala Mackermal heard of the purchase of the horse he seemed very much embarrassed, but what could he do? He returned next day and brought me a message from the governor couched in the sweetest words. He said that he could no longer suppress those sentiments of friendship that he entertained for me, and that no impediment any longer existed to the fulfilment of his desire to have me in his immediate neighbourhood. He had ordered a barrack to be prepared, and begged me to fix my dwelling there, as the Schalimar was too distant to allow him to establish that familiar intercourse that he wished should exist between us. I was also informed that the horse, which a little while before I had wished to buy, was now at my disposal; and that there were many horses in the city belong ing to the Schaykh Sahab, which should be sent to me, &c.

What in the commencement had been annoying, now became child's play; and though I did not like the idea of leaving the Schalimar, I made no objection, sent back a sweet-worded answer, and transferred the care of overseering the removal of my goods to responsible persons. On the appointed day I entered Kashmir. It was quite a festival for my health; with every breath I seemed to inhale new life, and feeling again the buoyant motion of a spirited horse, all my energies were aroused, and I enjoyed existence. I really believe that the pleasure one feels in the re-possession of returning health, indemnifies a man for the weary days he has passed on a bed of sickness.

Communications between me and the governor were now carried on more freely. Mackermal's interference was no longer necessary; and he was now often seen groping about in the dusk of the evening with the old sharper, Chuni Lahl, no doubt framing new snares, and bewailing the failure of their former plots.

The nights were beginning to be very cold, and even during the day, notwithstanding the sunshine and the cloudless sky, I often longed for the fire-side, a luxury unknown in the plains of India. My new dwelling had, according to the fashion of the country, windows of wooden net-work, which in summer admitted the air freely; but in winter these were covered with paper, which excluded the wind, without shutting out the light. By the use of these contrivances, I made myself as comfortable as I could, and soon found myself quite at home.

A few days after my arrival at my new abode, the old sinner, Chuni Lahl, entered with chattering teeth. He had just left the durbar or levee; he was evidently dismayed, and beckoning to my munschi, retired into an adjoining apartment. In a few minutes the munschi returned, and with a countenance full of terror, whispered in my ear that the maha-rajah had been murdered; that this account had come from Lahore, and that the Schaykh Sahab had commissioned Chuni Lahl to communicate the intelligence to me in the gentlest manner. This was, indeed, bad news. Chuni Lahl was questioned further: he told all he knew, how an insurrection had occurred at Lahore, during which the maha-rajah was murdered. He added that it was still kept a profound secret in Kashmir, as nobody knew what the consequences might be, and the governor was very much alarmed, for he was aware that the intelligence could not be much longer suppressed. Scarcely had Chuni Lahl departed, when all my servants entered; they had heard what had occurred at Lahore, and were in great consternation. The military guard that had accompanied me from Lahore, did not seem to know what to do; but as, in such circumstances, people generally think there is safety in numbers, they all came to the resolution of supporting me, and sharing my fate, whatever it might be.

A revolt of the military was apprehended in Kashmir: there were two parties in the province. The governor was suspected of being an instrument of Gulab Singh's, and it was supposed that the troops he commanded would join him. The military commander, on the contrary, adhered to his duty, and supported the royal party. The governor felt himself in a state of uncertainty and insecurity. His proceedings might, at any moment, call forth the resistance of the military commander, the consequence of which would be an *émeute* in Kashmir. I was assured that the governor sat in his divan, waiting the issue of events, with three sabres by his side. Whether this supply of arms was meant to inspire his enemies with fear, or himself with courage, I cannot say. The captain of my guard and several of his soldiers stood by me, declaring their devotedness to my service, and protesting that they were ready to defend the barrack in which we were staying, to the last man.

It was mid-day when the sad intelligence of Scheer Singh's death was communicated to me; in the evening Chuni Lahl returned. He had been again in the durbar, and so great was his terror, that he was now pliant as a worm. Mackermal was with him. The commander of my sepoys had been out, seeking intelligence amongst the royal party. What he learned corresponded with what I had been already told; but in addition, he found that the maharajah's death had been known to the Schayk Sahab two days before he divulged it. During this time, he had been endeavouring to obtain possession of the fort, but failed. The intelligence having travelled through another channel from Lahore, he was obliged to announce it publicly.

Chuni Lahl gave no further information concerning the murder of Scheer Singh by the Sandiwalia. The sirdars of the family of Sandiwalia, that is to say, the two brothers, Attar Singh, Ajid Singh, and the uncle Lehna

Singh, had formerly supported the rani, Karrak Singh's widow, and the two former had gone on her behalf to Calcutta, to obtain the support of the English government for the rani against Scheer Singh. When Scheer Singh took possession of the throne, the agent of the governor-general wrote to him in favour of Attar Singh who was in Calcutta, advancing the interests of the rani. This letter assured Scheer Singh that he might trust to Attar's fidelity, and that the latter would never again undertake any thing against him. In consequence of this interposition, Attar Singh was recalled, Scheer Singh loaded him with presents, and from that time forward there was nothing in their conduct towards each other, that could give suspicion of the existence of ill-feeling.

Amongst the Hindoos of the warrior class, the Dhassera festival is considered the most solemn of the year. It was instituted in remembrance of the rani's expedition against Lanka. This feast is observed with great ceremony by the Sikhs. It is celebrated on New Year's Day, and forms an epoch in their reckoning of time. The military advance from every quarter towards Lahore, and all classes present valuable gifts to the maha-rajah.

A short time before my arrival at Kashmir, presents of valuable shawls, and gold and silver had been sent to Lahore for the Dhassera. Everything had been arranged with great pomp in Lahore, the troops were drawn out, and the festive ceremonies had already commenced. The Maha-rajah Scheer Singh, had entered the palace Schab-Lahore, and was holding a durbar there, when the Sirdar, Ajid Singh Sandwalia, appeared with his uncle, Lehna Singh, at the head of his regiment, under pretence of exercising his men in the presence of the maha-rajah. Ajid Sing entered the durbar, and requested the maha-rajah to step into an adjoining chamber, from whence he could see the movements of the troops. Scheer Singh arose, went into the next chamber, and took his place at the window. Ajid Singh had also told him that he had been lately at Ludianah, and had brought a double-barrelled rifle, and asked permission to show it to the maha-rajah. The rifle was brought, and whilst Scheer Singh was standing at the window, Ajid discharged two balls in his back.

His son, Pertab Singh, a boy of thirteen, shared the same fate. Of the consequences of these assassinations, there had been yet no positive account.

I do not forget that I am only writing a journal, and that it is not my province to arrange events in historical succession. I insert the information and letters as I receive them. Chuni Lahl and Mackermal came often with intelligence of what they had heard, but they seemed much more anxious to hear than to narrate. The officers of the guard that accompanied me from Lahore, proved most faithful, and testified for me a sympathy that in the earlier period of our acquaintance, they had not displayed.

The intelligence from the city was far from being tranquillizing, and some of the reports concerned myself personally. It appeared that all parties had a dislike to me as being an European, and thought this a favourable opportunity to give vent to their feelings. The people, that is the class we so designate in Europe, did not participate in this sentiment: they are too sharp-sighted not to perceive that the European rule would be less oppressive than that of their native princes. The governors of provinces and their underlings in office, are those who most dislike Europeans.

This desire to slack their thirst for vengeance, was counterbalanced by the fear infused by rumours then abroad. People spoke of the English invading the Punjab; and some talked of an army of sixty thousand men drawn up on the banks of the Sutlej, and under these circumstances, no one wished to take upon himself the responsibility of offering violence to a European. There were other considerations. In case of an outbreak which seemed unavoidable, keeping me a prisoner might be turned to some advantage. The governor, Gulam Muhyiddin, also feared that I might join with a portion of the nobles, who would thus find an easier medium of communication with the English, and that this connection might end in an invasion of Kashmir.

The governor had, from the beginning, used every effort to prevent my coming in contact with persons of that class, and during my residence at the Schalimar, whenever a sirdar showed a friendly feeling towards me, a stop was soon put to all intercourse between us. Perhaps the hatred against the governor which pervaded every class in Kashmir from the beggar to the sirdar was the occasion of this; perhaps it was a precaution dictated by a bad conscience, or perhaps it was in compliance with the wishes of Gulab Singh, the Rajah of Jumbu, brother to to the Vizier Dehan Singh, and who is one of the most powerful rulers in the mountain districts.

CHAPTER II.

Gulab Singh—Not a friend to the English—His designs on Kashmir—Threatened attempt on my life—An excursion to Islamabab—Attack upon my luggage—Chuni Lahl becomes my Akbar Navis—Letters from Lahore—An account of Scheer Singh's death—Pertab Singh and Dehan Singh are assassinated—Murder of Misser Beli Rahm.

Gulab Singh is one of the most remarkable characters in the country. He is the declared enemy of the Europeans, for the simple reason that they are the great impediment to the accomplishment of his projects. He rules, so to say, Kashmir; and the oppression that prevails here, though quite conformable to the sentiments of Gulam Muhyiddin, originates with Gulab Singh. With deep-laid policy, he governs the provinces under his own immediate rule with justice and lenity, for he wishes to be held in good repute; but those governors over whom his influence extends, he induces to act with harshness and severity.

I have had in later years frequent opportunities of conversing with persons holding situations under the Indo-English Government, and they have always spoken of Gulab Singh with the highest esteem, and said that he had afforded the English the greatest assistance in the Khyber pass, where it would have been easy for him to destroy the whole army without exposing himself to the slightest suspicion. Gulab Singh is looked upon as the hero of the Punjab, the support and security of the European influence in this part of India. These are the opinions held on the south of the Sutlej; but the natives think differently. Even his services in the Khyber pass they do not rate so highly, and seem to think that his conduct there was perfectly in conformity with his own private plans. As a consequence of his designs on Kashmir, he naturally regarded the Affghans as his enemies, and as to an act of treachery towards the English, he was too well watched by Avitabelli to allow the possibility of that, even if such a proceeding had not been inimical to his own projects. Deceiving the English army at that time would not have destroyed the English power, but would have obliged the Maha-rajah of Lahore to declare war against him, a circumstance that would have averted the present catastrophe of which he was the author. It may be said of this man, that he is the terror of the children and the torturer of the grown-up people of Kashmir. How often have my people, around the crackling fire, when assured that the ear of no spy was listening, for hours together, told us of this tyrant, this betrayer, to whom no duty, no promise, no sorrow was sacred—who cared for no human being, and who spared not even the blood of his own kindred. The Schaykh, Gulam Muhyiddin, was his instrument, his creature: crafty and unprincipled in the extreme, he was just the man for his service. Munschi Mackermal or Lala Mackermal, a Pandit from the mountains, was an agent of Gulab Singh, and my mehmendar from Lahore. Chuni Lahl, a Brahmin from the neighbourhood of Saharempur, was, as he afterwards admitted, a dependant of the Vizier Dehan Singh, of Mera Singh, and of Gulab Singh, who formed, indeed, a precious triumvirate. The family of Gulab and Dehan Singh are Radjputs, and on this account the Sikhs are well inclined towards them. Though their creatures are for the most part Hindoos and Mahomedans; there are, certainly some Sikhs amongst them, in whom, however, their masters do not seem to place such implicit confidence.

Gulab Singh is sensible enough not to seek to extend his power in a direction where he may lose all. He wishes for the mountain districts and for Kashmir, he could then laugh at the masters of the lower provinces. He wishes to avoid coming in contact with the English power, and looks northwards towards Thibet and Chinese Tartary, where he thinks he could extend his conquests without dread of European interference. He would sell the Punjab ten times over to the English to serve his own purpose, and would betray the English then, did he find a profit in so doing. The natives in the northern province maintain that the English are not acquainted with his character, or that they would not for one day keep up a friendly intercourse with him.

Amongst the many agents that Gulab Singh employed here, I will only mention those immediately connected with myself. In the many complicated arrangements that were made in my establishment, Mackermal took occasion to introduce an under-munschi, named Uttumjin, a man who had once been well-off in the world, but who was now forced into a subordinate position, and was dependant on Mackermal; still, in the absence of his master, he sometimes ventured to deviate from his instructions. Things were in this state at the time of the outbreak at Lahore. The entire catastrophe had been known to Schaykh Gulam Muhyiddin, who was in Gulab Singh's confidence, and there can be no doubt that he intended to seize Kashmir, had the aspect of affairs been favourable. In order to forward these views, it would be necessary that Dehan Singh should continue in his office of vizier, and still guide the helm of affairs. This most important condition was wanting, which was particularly perplexing to

Gulam Muhyiddin, because his son Iman was, according to the custom of the country, kept a prisoner at Lahore, as a hostage for his father's fidelity. Dehan Singh was on good terms with Gulam Muhyiddin, and while he lived, Iman was safe; but things had changed, and Gulam Muhyiddin's son was closely watched at Lahore.

If one might venture to draw a conclusion from detached circumstances, one would be inclined to say that General Ventura was no stranger to the proceedings at Lahore, though he might not participate in them, a possibility that I could never admit. It was evident that Gulam Muhyiddin was *très lié* with General Ventura, but there were many grounds for this intimacy. The safety of Iman Muhyiddin might have formed the subject of their intercourse, or commercial transactions might have been its groundwork; but it never appeared that General Ventura and Gulab Singh were private acquaintances.

From what has been said, it might be expected that I should be able to give a detailed explanation of the events that were passing around, but I am far from being in a position to do so. There is a mystery and a stillness about state events in India, that almost preclude the possibility of discovering who are the real actors. A circumstance, trifling in itself, may serve to give a better idea of the character of the people, than long discourses could do.

Since I had succeeded in procuring a horse, I was in the habit of riding out in the evening, and returning about sunset to supper. On the day on which I had learned more detailed particulars concerning the events at Lahore, the naib, or captain of my body-guard, came and advised me not to ride out that evening, as there was a report in circulation that there was a plot laid to cut me down near a certain bridge that I was in the habit of passing. This was not very agreeable intelligence: still I was determined not to give up my evening ride, come what would.

I set out at the usual hour, and passed unmolested the spot where I had expected to find an executioner. There were a few persons there: I rode quietly by. I, however, took the precaution of returning by a different route.

My people were greatly delighted at my safe arrival, a good deal, I think, upon their own account. In the morning I was told that I had had a narrow escape; that the design against my life was not yet abandoned, and that my next evening's excursion might bring fatal consequences. My naib, as well as two others, brought me this intelligence. The inhabitants of Kashmir are, so to say, women; and according to the accounts given here, either Ackbar or Jehanghir condemned them to wear female costume, from which time their ancient valour and spirit declined, the petticoat, it is supposed, having infected them with feminine pusillanimity. To apprehend a serious attack from such creatures, would have been ridiculous: they neither possessed weapons, nor courage to use them. The soldiers in Kashmir were not to be feared; they were supporters of the government, to which party I belonged; it was only the creatures of Gulab Singh who could be suspected of entertaining a design against me.

On the following morning I solicited an audience of the governor. He was very much excited; his whole appearance betrayed the uneasiness of his mind. He promised me all the security that it was in his power to afford; but he did not know whether he was himself safe; every hour might bring a change. It was agreed that I should send letters to Lahore, and that I should not leave Kashmir until I received positive intelligence that I was expected in the Punjab. He further advised me not to make a journey through Attok to Peshawur, on account of the insecurity of the roads; and lastly, that I should not leave the city until we received better news; and that, in the meantime, I could see the country around, and make an excursion to Islamabad.

In the evening, I rode out at the usual hour. The windows were crowded with heads; all eyes were turned upon me with eager curiosity; but no harm befel me. The following morning, everything was prepared for my departure. My luggage and servants, with the exception of two, were sent by water; and with the two remaining servants, and escorted by the thanadar and kharidar of the district, I set out on horseback. The state of things in the city, or rather the relations between the governor and

Whares Khan, the commander of the troops, were not very satisfactory. The fort was closed, well furnished with provisions, and all communication with the town cut off. The governor felt very uncomfortable, for the cannon of the fort commanded the whole town. There were some soldiers of Gulab Singh's in the city, and a large body of troops was expected within a few days. In the meantime, negociations were to be entered into, to try to induce Whares Khan to surrender the fort and join the governor's party.

The day was beautiful, and my spirits rose as I found myself again on the march over flood and field. The land was well cultivated, and presented a smiling aspect. Beguiling the way with song and story, we had travelled during about two hours, when one of my servants came running towards us. He said that at a little distance on the other side of the river, my boat had been forcibly seized, and the luggage carried off. My first inquiry was for the thanadar and kharidar, and we immediately agreed to hurry to the scene of action. When we arrived we found the boat empty, some of my people were standing beside it, others had gone into the village. The principal inhabitants of the village were called, and the thanadar simply told them that if they did not replace the stolen property in the boat within a certain time, all should be punished, and the village taxed to the value of what had been taken. The villagers protested their ignorance of the fate of the missing property, and swore that there was neither chest nor pack in the village. But the thanadar was firm, and within half an hour the boat was re-laden with great care, and even better packed than it had been originally.

I now proceeded undisturbed, and was able to enjoy the air, the purity and balmy freshness of which nothing could excel. It is this ambrosial air, undoubtedly, that has won for Kashmir the reputation of having been the earthly paradise. The land, however fertile, is not unmatched; for other climes can show as fair a soil, as lovely a landscape; but over no other country does such an atmosphere hover as over that sweet valley, placed amongst those high mountains, that shelter it from the rude storm, whilst they lift it nearer to the unclouded sun.

And so it is, the valley of Kashmir is not very high above the level of the sea—not more than between five thousand and five thousand four hundred feet, a height which would not alone be sufficient to procure it the delicious climate it enjoys, were it not surrounded by those high mountains that, defending the valley from the cold blast of the north, exclude the burning winds of the south, or, at least, cool them in their passage.

I arrived in Islamabad, which I found a wretched place: the second city in Kashmir seemed to me no more than a village. My dwelling was a filthy abode, and when, after much cleaning and sweeping, and laying of carpets, it was transformed into something tolerable, and a pleasant fire lighted, out crept numbers of scorpions, anxious to enjoy the comfortable blaze; and they stirred about with an activity that one would never give them credit for, from their ordinary lazy habits.

Chuni Lahl had accompanied me on my journey, but he now began to express a desire to return to Kashmir. So far from opposing this wish, I indirectly encouraged it, for I was glad to get rid of the sneaking fellow. I told him that it would be very desirable for me to have a person in Kashmir that I could trust, who would report to me everything that might occur in my absence, and who would support my interest with the government. I will here make a remark for the benefit of those who are not acquainted with Indian customs. It is a practice with all those who are in connection with the native governments, to place a news-writer, or akbar navis, at the court, and this man gives them information of all that passes there. They also present their master's letters to the authorities, and support his interests as far as they can. These akbar navises are recognized by the government; they are introduced by their masters, and are accepted, or if not liked, a request is made that another should be chosen.

The recent occurrences made it desirable for me to have a person at the Court of Kashmir, who could give me intelligence of the proceedings there, and the proposition of installing

Chuni Lahl in the capacity of akbar navis was alike agreeable to him and to the Schaykh Sahab. That these akbar navises are persons of some influence is quite evident, and they are often connected with a deep system of bribery, and it sometimes happens that the employer, instead of having a person at the court who will advance his interest, finds, too late, that he has intrusted his secrets to a man who is not incapable of selling them for gold.

My affairs at the Court of Kashmir were not of sufficient importance to require an akbar navis to represent my interests; but, as I have said, I wished to know what was going on, and as the opportunity presented itself so favourably, I profited by it to get rid of Chuni Lahl, who returned willingly to Kashmir to enjoy his new honours. Mackermal had remained at Kashmir, but had sent his underling, Uttumjin, to attend me. In his master's absence he did not make the same pretensions, and was therefore less importunate to me.

Islamabad has some shawl-looms, but of an inferior description. My next inquiry was as to the probability of enjoying a hunt, and on this subject the most flattering hopes were given me, all of which were disappointed.

I received some akbars from Chuni Lahl, which I will here transcribe, as they will serve to give a clear idea of the state of the city. The same halkar (letter-bearer) brought me a letter from Lala Hascrindas, the akbar navis of the English Government at Lahore. Here is the letter of Hascrindas :

" I hope that Hasur (your Grace) has received the letters that I have already sent. The following is a correct account of the events that have occurred here. On the 15th September, 1843, the Maha-rajah Scheer Singh went to Schabelaur, and held a durbar. Sirdar Ajid Singh and Sirdar Lehna Singh came to the maha-rajah, and prayed him to be so good as to inspect their regiments. The maha-rajah rose immediately, and went to see the troops. Sirdar Ajid Sandiwalia fired at Scheer Singh with a double-barrelled gun, by reason of which the maha-rajah gave up the ghost. All the regiments that belonged to the Sandiwalia fired with their carabines and guns. Many of the maha-rajah's munschis were shot at the same time as he. Ajid Singh assembled his troops, and proceeded amid beating of drums to the fort. Sirdar Lehna Singh went into the garden of Sirdar Desha Singh, where he murdered Pertab Singh with a sword, and then coming to the fort, entered with Ajid Singh. Rajah Dehan Singh was in the fort. The sirdars gave it as their opinion, that if Dehan Singh were not killed, he would domineer over us and the country, so that we ought to kill him, and hereupon Dehan Singh was murdered. When the rajahs heard this, they were all very angry. They went with the Rajah Hera Singh to storm the fort with cannon, and on the evening of the 16th September the fort was taken. Rajah Hera Singh, Sutjed Singh, Raa Kessari Singh and Misser Lahl Singh were all engaged in the storming of the fort.

"On the 17th, Rajah Hera Singh placed Rajah Dalib Singh on the throne. A salute of seven rounds was fired by the cavalry and infantry regiments in the service of the Rajah Sahab, and all was peace at Lahore. All prepared with uniforms, &c., for the celebration of the Dhassera feast. The troops were to be reviewed in the Schani-mia-mir, where the presents for the Dhassera should be also received."

I will add a few particulars transmitted to me from Lahore, and not contained in the above letter. With the maha-rajah, his friend, the Sirdar Budh Singh, had been murdered. Immediately on this event, Lehna Singh went into the garden where, according to custom, the crown prince was giving presents of cows to the Brahmins. The prince had been appointed to discharge this office, which is considered very honourable, and in the fulfilment of his duties he was placed upon the gatti, or seat of honour. The Sandiwaliy are the nearest relatives of the maha-rajah, and as such are treated by them with great respect. As soon as Pertab Singh saw Lehna Singh approaching, he rose from his seat and advanced some steps to meet him. Holding out his hand, he said: "Come, uncle, sit beside me, and distribute the presents." Lehna Singh, unmoved by this affectionate reception, drew his sword, and with two blows cut off Pertab's head, which he wrapped in his shawl and carried off.

As Ajid Singh was on his way to the fort he met Dehan Singh, who was coming to learn the success of the affair. Dehan Singh was in a chariot, and Ajid proposed that he should mount a horse; this the other at first refused, and Ajid Singh represented to him that his appearance on horseback would make a much better impression on the troops. Upon this he got on horseback, and both proceeded to the fort. Here they met Lehna, who showed Dehan, Pertab's head. Others say that the boy's head was thrown into Dehan Singh's chariot, that he seemed very much shocked, and that it was then he refused to quit his chariot, but afterwards yielded to the representations made to him. Dehan Singh rode beside Ajid Singh to the castle; just as they arrived there, a shot was fired that pierced Dehan Singh in the back. "Villain," he exclaimed, and drawing his sword turned upon Ajid Singh, but at the same moment a number of shots were fired, and Dehan Singh fell dead from his horse. The Sandiwaliy were now masters of the fort, into which they with their troops, to the amount of five or six hundred men, retired.

When Hera Singh heard of the death of his father, he fled for refuge to the little fort of General Avitabelli, who was not at that time in the Punjab. Here Hera Singh harangued Avitabelli and Court's regiments. He told them of Scheer Singh's death, reminded them that he had been reared by Runjeet Singh, who had always treated him as his child, and that Scheer Sing had ever looked upon him as a brother. He then painted his sorrow at the murder of his benefactor, and asked the troops would they revenge his assassination? If they wished for vengeance, he bid them follow him: if not, then he should only retire. The troops declared for Hera Singh, as did also General Ventura, who with his regiments was in the place.

In the evening they assembled, and during the night entered the town. It is not to be wondered at that some bazaars were plundered. At midnight the moon shone forth, and favoured by her light, the troops attacked the fortress. At two o'clock the following afternoon, a breach was made, and the fort was stormed on two sides; those inside the walls lost courage, and drew back. Ajid Singh tried to escape, and attempted to let himself down by a rope on the northern side, into the moat beneath. The rope broke, he fell, and being corpulent could not recover his balance. He was made prisoner, his head cut off and brought to Hera Singh. His headless body was hanged, with that of his accomplice Meil Kesita, before the city gate. Both shared the same scaffold, and were hanged by the feet.

Lehna Singh was sought during a long time in the fortress; he was at length discovered in a hiding-place. Seeing his enemies before him, he sprang up, and defended himself so bravely that none could approach. At length the bow and arrow were brought, and many a shaft was fired before he fell. His body was afterwards hanged before the city gate called the Kashmir Derwasa.

The next thought of the troops was to plunder the treasure chamber; in this they succeeded, many leaving their weapons behind, and taking off the booty. These occurrences gave rise to many bloody scenes. It was said that many of the sirdars participated in the robbery; amongst these was Gurmuk Singh, one of the chief Sikh princes, to whose custody the crown prince had been intrusted, and who, it is said, was formerly accused of having been concerned in a plot against the minister's life. This assertion must, however, be received with great caution, as Bhai Gurmuk Singh was the personal enemy of Hera Singh, who profited by this opportunity to wreak his vengeance on him. Bhai Gurmuk Singh was the head of the Sikh princes, and as such obnoxious to the Radjput Dehan Singh and his consorts. Through him they had to fear the opposition of the Sikhs, and by his death their greatest enemy was removed. To form a pretext for attacking him, the report of his robbing the treasury was promulgated, though if Gurmuk Singh laid his hand on the treasures, it was probably with the intention of saving them from the Radjputs. The cruelty that was exercised against him proves that his death was the fruit of private malice. He offered forty lacs of rupees for his life; it was refused. An iron ring was passed through his jaws, near the root of the tongue; by this he was swung round, and then barbarously put to death.

The same fate befel the treasurer, Misser Beli Rahm, he who had shown me the crown jewels. His brothers and cousins were cut in pieces and thrown into the river.

CHAPTER III.

Fresh accounts from Lahore—Dalib Singh made King—Hera Singh becomes Vizier—Akbar from Chuni Lahl—Akbar from Lahore—Excursion to Schahabad—Scarcity of game—The Thanadar—His hospitality—Dancing girls—Anecdotes of Runjeet Singh—His artifices to obtain money.

I RECEIVED intelligence from Lahore, that the Dhassera festival, at which so many disturbances had been expected, passed off very well, a circumstance mainly attributable to the precautions taken by General Ventura. The letter continues: "We have now our young king Dalib Singh; he is about eight years of age. The young Rajah, Hera Singh, is vizier in his father's place. It is said that the Rajah Dehan

Singh had conspired with the Sandiwaliy to assassinate Scheer Singh, but the minister wished to put the crown prince, Pertab Singh, upon the throne, that so he might himself virtually hold the reins of government; but the Sandiwaliy entertained a different design, and wished to reign themselves with Dalib Singh on the throne. The Sandiwaliy had promised the troops four months pay, as a gratuity, if they supported them; but Hera Singh induced the soldiers to join his party, telling them that the Sandiwaliy intended to give up the country to the English. The troops, in joining Hera Singh, made certain conditions: he should give one month's pay to all the soldiers, to those who were on leave of absence, as well as those who were in the city; and those who, hitherto, had received eight rupees, should in future receive twelve. They have already begun to make payments; the finances are very low, and, in this case, nothing remains for Hera Singh but to escape into his native mountains. I have heard that General Ventura will follow Generals Court and Avitabelli, and leave the country. General Avitabelli is certainly still in

Amballa, and promises to return, as it is said, if his present pay, fifty thousand rupees yearly, will be increased. He also requires a greater extension of power. Perhaps these are only pretences. General Court is evidently waiting the decision of General Avitabelli. Should things not turn out as they wish, both will go to Calcutta. General Ventura told me that it was his opinion that within a year and a half, no European would be in service here, for the rajah hates them. Everything is at present quiet, and will continue so as long as money is scattered freely, but there is no time to be lost," &c.

Chuni Lahl writes as follows:

"From the day that Hasur (your Grace) arrived here in Kashmir, I have always been well. A few days since I went to see Kier Bamana, and returned on Monday. A paper has arrived from Lahore, which Hasur will receive with this letter; it gives an account of the events that occurred in Lahore. According to the information of some persons, everything is quiet in the land of Kalsaj. Everyone can pass unmolested through the streets, and in safety along the roads, under the protection of Saad Gru.

" Rajah Hera Singh has made the best arrangements suitable to the customs of the country, and everything is as before: it is even better. He gives presents to the sirdars, and everyone performs his service with pleasure. Hasur will be graciously pleased to answer this letter."

The akbar from Lahore contained the following. This is an akbar from the durbar bull and high council.

" In the morning Hera Singh awoke and washed and dressed himself, and went with his elephants to the fort; and in Bara Dery in Hasuri Bagh he held a council, and at the same time Raa Kessra Singh, Mia Allab Singh, Sirdar Lehna Singh Mushidia, Sirdar Seham Singh Artariwalia, Divan Dinanath, Bachschi Backed Rahm, and other nobles, and civil and military officers, were present, and offered their gifts. After this, Hera Singh called together Rajah Suddhed Singh, Sirdar Lehna Singh, and Ventura Sahab, and these advised him; and it was determined that the soldiers' pay should be raised, so that those who before had received seven rupees per month should receive three additional; and those who got eight and a half should have an addition of two and a half; and those who before had received nine should now get eleven rupees. Hera Singh said:

" 'As I promised you, so have I done. You are now to fulfil your service under the commands of your officers with sincerity, and to follow your commanders, and he who does not obey his officers is guilty.'

"Upon this the assembled regiments cried out: 'Hohd adja!' very well.

"After this, he commanded the kharidars to make the following payments:

"To Schaykh Iman Muhyiddin 2 lacs of rupees; Rajah Gulab Singh, 1 lac of rupees; Misser Belli Rahm, 50,000 rupees; Lala Rahm Deal, 25,000 rupees; Bora Hai Singh, 15,000 rupees; Rahm Schadi, 50,000 rupees.

"After Hera Singh had given these commands concerning the money, he betook himself to his house and slept.

"*5th Assud.* Rajah Hera Singh awoke and washed and dressed himself, and went in his chariot to the fort, and took with him Rajah Dalieb Singh. He then mounted his elephant, and went to Anarkali, to show him the troops, and to see the exercises. As he arrived at Anarkali, General Ventura Sahab fired the cannon, and his regiments presented arms. After the maha-rajah had seen these exercises he was pleased, and distributed presents. To Allahi Bachsch, 250 rupees; to Frannond Munschi a pair of white shawls, and 100 rupees to each regiment; and from that he went to the fort, and having arrived there, the Maha-rajah Dalib Singh went into his sleeping apartment, and Rajah Sahab into the council.

"Lehna Singh Muhidia, Ventura Sahab, Rajah Sudjid Singh, Mia Allab Singh, Raa Kessra Singh, Diwan Dinanath, and those persons who come here every day, proceeded to the discharge of their duties. At the same time news arrived from Peshawur, that through the good management of Sirdar Akal Puruckja there is peace. The akbar navis of Cabul is in Peshawur, and says that the zemindars in Atte Say showed symptons of revolt, upon hearing the events that occurred at Lahore. On this account, Sirdar Fedsch Singh has ordered two regiments to be sent there, and Sirdar Dog Mohamed Khan, and Mahomed Akbar Khan are as usual in Cabul, and have sent letters of condolence to Hera Singh. It is, however, said, that at the fid (festival) Akbar Khan will come with five thousand sawars and four pieces of cannon, to Schahabad. After this, every one who had horses belonging to Gurmuk Singh, brought them before the Rajah Hera Singh. He ordered them to be brought to Mium Backun Khan, Darogha of the horse, and the bearer said that they were good; and other things were brought from Gurmuk Singh. It was ordered that Raa Kessra Singh and Diwan Dinanath should sit down, and write these things of him, and then give it to Misser Lal Singh Dosh Khana. And these answered: 'hohd adja,' (very well.) Afterwards he received the presents of the regiment Tanggoi, and raised the pay of each sepoy to five rupees. And two cannon were brought, which had belonged to Bai Gummuk Singh, and Hera Singh ordered them to be given to Sirdar Lehna Singh. He afterwards ordered that the camp for the artillery should be fixed near the camp of Colonel Allahi Bachoch's artillery. After this he dismissed all, and went to sleep.

"This day the 6th. Rajah Hera Singh left his

house, and got upon the roof, where he ordered the derwar to be assembled. In this assembly there appeared, Sirdar Attar Singh Kaliwalia, Sirdar Lehna Singh, Sirdar Futhe Singh Mahn, Sirdar Krishen Singh, son of a Jemedar, Ventura Sahab, Court Sahab, Diwan Dinanath, Diwan Ajudia Bersad, Rajah Sudjed Singh.

"Court Sahab said, that Avitabelli Sahab was in Simla, and intended to go to Ferozepoor. It would be necessary to give him a perwanah to Sirdar Scham Singh Atturiwalia, and another for provisions on his journey. Hera Singh gave directions to Diwan Dinanath to write the perwanahs. A letter was brought from Sirdar Ladtha Singh, saying that the son of Bai Gurmuk Singh had retired into his house with a hundred soldiers, and would not surrender. Ladtha Singh had ordered the city gates to be closed, and the house to be watched. He concluded with: 'Whatever you order, I will do.' Hera Singh answered: 'There shall be four pieces of cannon directed against the house, it shall be destroyed; the son of Gurmuk Singh shall be taken prisoner, and all the members of the family driven from the city, and thou—Ladtha Singh—shalt thyself perform this duty.'

"Hera Singh went to Hassuri Bagk, the garden in the first courtyard. He remained here a short time. He afterwards went forth with Sirdar Lehna Singh and Pandit Schella, mounted his chariot, and drove to Mia Mir, received the presents of his troops, spoke to them words of kindness, and gave 500 rupees to the infantry and 100 to the artillery. It was now noon, and he retired to his house and slept."

Besides these letters, I received daily information of what was passing, either through the voice of rumour, or through the medium of private letters. To narrate all these would be to eke out my journal to an unpardonable length. Some of these reports were probable, others quite the contrary.

It was said that Hera Singh had seized on all the possessions of the Sandiwaliy, that several overseers of provision magazines had retired without leave, and that yet no deficiency had been found in the stores. A very improbable report was, that two English gentlemen had arrived at Lahore, with presents for the Maha-rajah, Dalib Singh; but that both, with their followers, had been cut down in an insurrection of the military. This was, of course, highly improbable; but I mention it merely to show the nature of the reports with which I was pestered, and to which the narrators generally contrived to give a colouring that bore some resemblance to the circumstances in which I was myself placed.

The Thanadar, Brehm Singh, induced me to undertake an excursion into the district Schahabad, where, he assured me, there was abundance of sport to be had in bear-hunting. I intended to fix my camp at Beremgalla, the most remote village of the district, and to remain there eight or ten days. When I arrived, the thanadar of the place assured me that there was not a bear in the entire district, and that Brehm Singh had sent me, only because he was his personal enemy. Brehm Singh is a Sikh, the Thanadar of Schahabad is a Pandit. I had here a good opportunity of learning the feelings with which I was viewed by many, whom the government pawanah obliged to become my hosts. I could not forbear letting Brehm Sing know how little I felt obliged at being induced to undertake this journey with a retinue of twenty-five servants, and between forty and fifty coolies, and to meet only disappointment. This was something like making an April fool of one.

As I was at the place, let the thing turn out as it would, I was determined to take a view of the environs. On the morning after my arrival, I set out for the forest, accompanied by a guide. At every half hour's ride from Beremfalla, I met little hamlets, consisting of a few small houses, until, after four hour's journey, I reach a few scattered dwellings, which, I was assured, formed the boundary of the cultivated land in that direction. These were inhabited by cowherds, who gave me the most minute details about the forests and the game they contained. I found in the cowherds a very friendly people, far preferable to those I had hitherto met in Kashmir. They are open-hearted, straightforward, kindly, and very obliging, without the sneaking civility that distinguishes the inhabitants of the valley. They offered to traverse the wood in their neighbourhood, hoping that they might be so fortunate as to find a bear; but they assured me that they had never yet seen one by day, though it sometimes happened that Mister Bruin came forth at night to steal their maize. Upon closer inspection, the traces of bears were found in the forest; but the cowherds were of opinion that there were not more than two or three in the entire mountain-range. The result of my search was, that I returned without the hope of enjoying a hunt.

If the Thanadar of Schahabad possessed little skill in matters appertaining to the chase, he was by no means a novice in housekeeping. The dwelling in which I was fixed was small certainly, but exquisitely neat. In the principal chamber—or, to speak more correctly, in the only chamber of this very small house—was a trelliced partition of wood, beautifully wrought; there were pretty pillars and arches of the same material. This is a peculiarity of structure in the Kashmerian houses. Part of my chamber was raised about two feet above the rest, the upper part being the place of honour. I spoke before of trellice-work of this kind being in the governor's palace in the city of Kashmir, but there it was, I believe, used merely as a partition.

The entertainment was in keeping with the comfort and excellence of the house. The dancing-girls appeared in the evening. They were far less bedecked and bedizened than those I was in the habit of seeing, and in many respects far preferable to their co-sisters in the large cities. They were simple in their dress, unaffected in their deportment, and showed in their whole bearing a maidenly reserve. These poor girls are the purchased property of certain persons in the district, who buy them in their infancy, and train them to this severe and ignoble mode of life. I asked one of them would she wish to leave her master, but she said no; that she had been sold when a child; that she knew no tie of kindred; she had not known the love of a parent. If she were now set free, whither could she turn? There was no home, no family to claim her, or whom she could claim, and that were she to leave her present employers, she should infallibly fall into the power of others. She said that she had no wish to travel into great cities; that her only desire was to live unnoticed in that retired district. She did not wish, she said, to draw attention to herself, and that my sympathy might bring unpleasant consequences. She added, that the people whose bread she had eaten were now old; that she owed them a debt of gratitude, and was willing to work for them. "Oh!" she exclaimed, "if the priests would only acknowledge that goodness and the love of the beautiful are planted in the hearts of men by God himself, and not through the oft unclean and mundane-minded priesthood!"

I returned somewhat sooner to Islamabad than the Thanadar, Brehm Singh, expected. The days passed tediously enough. I had not yet given up all idea of the chase, and was making preparations for a hunt. The evenings were passed at the fireside, which the chilliness of the season made very agreeable. Seated at my hearth, I enjoyed the society of the patriarchs of Islamabad, who beguiled the night with many a legendary tale. The conversation sometimes turned upon Runjeet Singh.* Many stories were told of him that would fall strangely upon European ears. A few of a less exceptionable character I shall insert here.

An English gentleman once asked Runjeet Singh, who was the Maha-rajah's vizier. "Myself," answered Runjeet. "And who is Rajah?" inquired the stranger. "Guru Nanak," was the answer.

Runjeet Singh was often in want of money; and the means with which his inventive spirit contrived to fill his coffers, were not always the most innocent. It is the custom in India to make presents to the master of the house upon the occurrence of any important event in the family, such as the birth or marriage of children, &c., the gift being always proportioned to the wealth of the giver.

One day, Runjeet Singh was riding through the town, revolving in his mind the ways and means of replenishing his treasury. His glance happened to fall upon a pretty little boy who

* Maha-rajah, Runjeet Singh, the celebrated founder of the present dynasty of the Punjab, was born in 1780. He was son to Maha Singh, grandson to Charat Singh.

was sitting in his father's shop. A lucky thought struck him—that little boy might be made a means of extricating him from his difficulties. He returned to his palace, sent for the boy and his father, and declared in full divan that it was his intention to adopt the child. This affiliation is by no means uncommon in India, and the boy's prepossessing appearance seemed to furnish sufficient grounds for the rajah's liking.

This increase in the rajah's family was made the occasion of great festivity. Rejoicings were made, and rich gifts poured in from all sides; congratulations were offered to the rajah upon the acquisition of a new son; the boy was seated beside his adopted father, and, no doubt looked upon that day as the commencement of a princely career for himself. But his hopes were deceived. No sooner were the presents received, than the boy was sent home, and Runjeet Singh never afterwards took the slightest notice of him or his family.

CHAPTER IV.

Anecdotes of Runjeet Singh continued—His gratitude to a poor woman — Fresh efforts to find game — Abundance of bears—Misery of the Kashmerians—Letters from Islamabad—Akbar from Chuni Lahl—Akbar from Lahore — Akbars from Peschawur and Kashmir — Return to Kashmir — Conduct of Lala Mackermal—Disturbances in my new dwelling.

RUNJEET SINGH once received a visit from some English gentlemen, and many nobles and princes of Affghanistan. Wishing to make an imposing appearance before his visitors, he privately assembled nearly two thousand dancing-girls and females of that class, and gave them military uniforms and arms. These regiments filled two hundred halls in the seray of the palace. All were astonished at this accession to the military force, and even the Sikhs themselves did not know how the rajah had enrolled these new regiments.

It happened once, before Runjeet was king, that he, with two sirdars, was travelling towards Attok, during a campaign. The three soldiers lay down at dusk, on the banks of the Indus, to sleep. During the night the waters rose, and overflowed the banks. The three sleepers became uncomfortable; Runjeet woke, and slily crept up on his two companions, so keeping himself dry until morning. At early dawn they proceeded on their way to Gushranwalla, where the army was encamped. As the three soldiers journeyed along, they were sore pressed with hunger, and stopping, they held council to consider what they should do. They were in the neighbourhood of the enemy, and one of them proposed that he should advance, and slipping in amongst the troops, mingle with the soldiers at the time that provisions should be distributed, and so receive a share. He made the attempt and succeeded. He returned and divided his rations with his companions.

Strengthened by this meal, the three companions continued their journey; but were again attacked by hunger. One of the sirdars offered to go into a neighbouring village, which was at that time in the possession of the enemy, and seek for something to eat. He did so, and met a woman carrying a great load of bread to labourers who were working in the fields. The sirdar told her that Runjeet Singh was outside the village, that he needed something to eat, and begged of her to carry him the bread. She complied, and Runjeet, said to her: "To-morrow, I will take your village, and you shall be repaid."

On the same evening Runjeet reached his camp, and the following day stormed and took the village. He gave this village with several others to the woman who had brought him the bread, and her descendants are still in possession of the same. Nay more, it is said that even after Runjeet became king, he never passed the village without visiting the woman, and eating bread with her. He inquired into her family affairs, whether her sons were obedient, &c., and never by any act, belied the gratitude that he first expressed to her.

Once when Runjeet Singh was badly off for money, he was lying upon a bed in his chamber. There was no one present but his two sons Karak Singh and Scheer Singh. They were employed in rubbing his limbs; he was paralysed.

"My sons," said the rajah, "you are exerting yourselves to procure me comfort, but if you would really console me, give me money; the want of that is the sole source of my maladies." Upon this, Karak Singh went and brought his father all his jewels, but Runjeet shook his head and said, "I do not wish for jewels, it is money I want." Karak retired, and brought his father one hundred and fifty rupees. Thereupon the father was very glad, and turning to Scheer Singh said: "Have you nothing to offer your father." And Scheer Singh replied: "It has ever been my constant prayer to God that my father might never want anything of me, but that I might rather ask of him." This anecdote was related by Scheer Singh himself, who thought the answer very witty. He was very much praised for his presence of mind, even by Runjeet Singh himself.

Munschi Uttumjin related how once on a march, Runjeet Singh found himself greatly perplexed; all his opium was consumed. Uttumjin happened to say, in hearing of Runjeet Singh, that he was sure that his uncle who was fond of opium had some about him, and that if the maha-rajah would have no objection to use it, he only waited his commands to fetch the drug.

The rajah asked if the opium were good, and being satisfied on this point, accepted it. On the following day he sent an order for one thousand rupees to Uttumjin.

I determined to make some serious efforts to get up a hunt, and for this purpose resolved to try the Berguna, or district of Dadschenbarra, but I was assured that this would be useless, and for the simple reason that as there were no trees there, neither could there be a forest, and consequently no bears. Disappointed in this direction, I turned towards Raverbarra, which as well as Dadschenbarra, lies in the valley, through which one of the high roads to Ladax leads. On the way to Ladax, we passed a Hindoo temple, and the abode of a fakir, situated near a well, in which were fish too sacred to be made the food of man.

At Raverbarra I was appointed a pleasant dwelling, consisting of one large hall on the ground floor, well built, dry and airy. The kharidar of the berguna, or district, seemed greatly shocked at my visit, and if he had not hated bears before, I am convinced that from that hour he conceived a mortal antipathy to them. If the thanadars and kharidars were not pleased at my coming, it was quite different with the humbler classes. They were glad to see those, who had persecuted them during the whole year, obliged to suffer some annoyance, and they were not sorry to see those before whom they were obliged to crouch, forced in turn to humble themselves. They hoped, moreover, to get some profitable little job, which the government could not tax.

The kharidars and other place-holders assured me, and swore, that there was not a bear in the district, and that they had never even seen one; but all this could not induce me to give up my project. I was too old a hunter to be deceived, and to my experienced eye the ground promised well. After combating during two days with false reports, I sallied forth, and had the good fortune to shoot a bear. This event immediately changed the aspect of affairs. It was suddenly discovered that bears were by no means rare visitors in the neighbourhood; and those who before had protested that they had never seen a bear, could scarcely restrain their impatience till the following morning, to accompany me to the chase and give all kinds of information. The bear had been so easily shot, that all were of opinion that we should have great sport; but the next day was a blank. The kharidar and his beadles, armed with whips and sticks, led out that morning forty drivers. These poor wretches are little better than slaves.

The bear that I shot, was a large black one, with white spots on the breast, a species common in the Himalaya. This was the largest of the kind I had ever seen. Besides this, there is another species, of the colour of the red fox, which is covered with thicker and finer hair than the black bear. However, I have only seen the skin of a red bear, never the living animal.

I fired two shots at the bear, after which he still advanced thirty-five paces, and fell. At a call, all the drivers rushed up, and commenced with their long sticks to belabour the poor brute, which they believed to be not yet quite dead. The sound of their repeated blows reminded me of the beating of a flail on a barn-floor; but the bear was dead, and their exertions were expended in vain.

I have been in many lands, but nowhere did the condition of the human being present a more saddening spectacle than in Kashmir. It vividly recalled the history of the Israelites under the Egyptian rule, when they were flogged at their daily labour by their pitiless task-masters. And here the same picture presents itself: man raises his hand against his fellow-man, and for no other object than to excite physical pain. This troop of forty peasants were called together by a beadle, and driven along like a herd of cattle, the keeper walking behind, and striking all within his reach. This slave-driver carried a peculiar kind of whip, woven after the fashion of the Russian knout, a little more pliant, and about a foot and a half in length. There were three or four thongs, each having a knot on the end. The handle was about a foot and a half long. The beadle carries this whip in his girdle, and when the opportunity occurs uses it, as a driver of cattle does his goad, and indeed I ought to say, that he makes opportunities rather than awaits them.

It would have been useless to remonstrate, nor had I a right to expect that these people should view things in the same light that I did. I bethought me of another means of inducing the slave-master to lay aside his thong. I took it in my hand, admired it for some time, and offered to buy it as a curiosity. The price asked was not extraordinary, and I should have been well pleased with my bargain, if the next stick that presented itself had not been used as a substitute. However, it was neither as long nor as pliant as the whip, and could not inflict so keen a stroke upon the naked shoulders of the poor creatures who were obliged to submit to the blow; so that, on the whole, something was gained.

A messenger brought me letters from Islamabad, where I had left the greater number of my people. These were communications and akbars from Chuni Lahl. My worthy representative at the Court of Kashmir scattered incense on all sides in the following manner.

"Schaykh Gulam Muhyiddin maintains excellent order in Kashmir, certainly the best for the safety of the country. There is very good news from Lahore concerning the government of Hera Singh, who has established good order and made excellent arrangements. He has given many presents to the troops; all are pleased; nor is he less watchful of the interests of the land-owners, but takes care of all. Letters have arrived from Peshawur from the governor Sirdar Deja Singh, demanding an increase of troops; but the answer he received was, that until he explained for what service he required these troops, they would not be sent. I, Chuni Lahl, will forward to Hasur any intelligence that I receive on this head."

The following is an akbar from Lahore:

"Kashmira Singh and Peschawur Singh* were

* Half brothers to Scheer Singh.

two days with Bera Singh. It was with the consent of the maha-rajah and Hera Singh that they came. Two days after their arrival in Lahore, Peschawur Singh learned that Kashmira Singh and Bera Singh were murdered. Kashmira Singh came and said that he wished to know how his brother had died, and that had he known that he was in danger of death, he would come and die with him.

"The following day, Hera Singh confirmed to Peschawur Singh, the jackiere which he possessed, and told this to the troops, and then went to his business.

"After the funeral ceremonies, there was a report spread among the troops that Peschawur Singh too was dead. The following day, the maha-rajah was to hold a review; the troops would talk of Peschawur, and say, 'Where is he.' These reports were in circulation; the maha-rajah heard them, and said that Peschawur Singh was not dead, but had gone to his government, and that on the day of the review he should be seen riding beside the maha-rajah on an elephant. But after saying these things to the officer, he did not go to the review. He issued a parwanah declaring that Peschawur Singh should be present, and explain everything to the regiments; and that when Peschawur would be present everything would be right—why not—and Mosser Fella could be questioned, and the rajah."

I received at the same time an akbar from Peshawur and Kashmir, of which I will here transcribe the contents.

"It is reported here that the Prince Cameran, ruler of Herat, has fled to Persia, on account of the tyranny of his brother, Yar Mahomed Khan. He went to seek the aid of the King of Persia. The Shah assembled many of his troops, and came with the Prince Cameran to Mushud, and wrote a letter to Yar Mahomed Khan to this effect:

"'Thou comest, come to me, I will make thee Mur Sirdar, great sirdar.'

"Yar Mahomed wrote this answer to the Shah.

"'When thou formerly tookest possession of Herat, and did destroy it, there was no peace between us, and all this happened through the simplicity of Cameran. Now we are all friendly together, and we have made Mahomet Ackbar Khan great sirdar amongst us. Thou mayest come here without danger, we fear nothing; but do not think that thou canst come as formerly. And this is the answer of Dost Mahomed Khan that he will make no compromise.'

"The Shah of Persia, upon hearing this, became very angry, and left Musud, and came to Herat. It is supposed that he will have possession of it, before the end of this month. I have seen this written in the Ackbar archives, of Cabul, but I know not whether it is true or false."

Before this letter reached me, I had learned from the Schaykh Sahab, that there was now no impediment to my return, but that, on the contrary, he daily heard something from Lahore concerning it. There was now nothing to delay me, and I wrote a letter fixing the day o my departure, and set off for Islamabad, which I left on the morning after my arrival, with five boats containing my luggage and suite, and after twelve days sailing reached the city of Kashmir.

The government of Lahore had sent me as memendar, Chuni Lahl, and the governor of Kashmir had appointed the oft-mentioned Mackermal to be my munschi. It was his duty to see that the physical wants of my people were supplied, as well as my own. He was to provide quarters, servants, soldiers, &c., and to take care that everything was properly arranged. He had received a letter, informing him of the day of my departure for Kashmir, and desiring that he should provide lodgings and every other necessary. This letter had been written by my munschi, and communicated to him by his devoted slave, munschi Uttumjin. When I arrived at Kashmir, expecting to find every thing ready for my reception, I was not a little surprised to learn that no house had been hired, that indeed here and there a vacant house had been seen, but that when Schayk Sahab was asked about them, he always replied "he shall come into the barrack."

Now, whilst waiting for his final answer, I went into Delawer Khan's gardens, and after waiting double the length of time that ought to have been necessary, I returned to my boat preferring to wait the issue of events there, rather than in the garden, where a very dirty building was the only shelter I could find. After some time munschi Uttumjin appeared, and declared, without much circumlocution, that I should yet have to wait a long time before a house could be found.

He then turned towards my munschi, and added, that I, like all persons who had others under their command, was full of whims and humours, and that he did not think it at all praise-worthy in me, that during the time of my illness at Schahabagk, I had several times refused to see Lala Mackermal, saying that, "I feel myself too weak to see him, a conversation of even a few minutes would fatigue me." This had happened at most but two or three times, during the period when I was really very ill.

After this expression of his feelings the offended munschi withdrew, saying that he had some visits to make. He gave the people of the boat an order for provisions, nor did he forget the soldiers, but he went off without giving my people anything, or offering an explanation of his conduct.

A short time after he had disappeared, Chuni Lahl came and told me that he hoped to be able to get a house. He took my munschi with him, and both returning after a short delay, in ten minutes more, I was settled in my house. My new dwelling was agreeably situated on the banks of the river, and though there was no garden attached, I felt that I was compensated for that privation by the delightful view that lay outstretched before my windows. The house was the property of a Pandit who, on account of some few hundred rupees that he owed the government, gave up his house, until his debt should be paid.

The house, before my arrival, had been inhabited by the son of the rajah, or, more properly, of the Nabob of Muzusserabad. This young man, who was about seventeen or eighteen years of age, had, upon receiving intelligence of the events that had occurred at Lahore, retired into the fort, or rather dwelling, of Schaykh Sahab, but some of his people still remained in the house in the city, which was now appointed for my abode. Those persons belonging to the nabob's son who had remained behind, received directions to retire into the adjoining houses; but on the evening of my arrival, one of them forced his way into my antechamber, accompanied by a sepoy of the governor's, asserting and maintaining that he had a right to do so, as it was his house. The sepoy said that he was come from the governor to desire me not to offer any annoyance to the people of the nabob, nor in any way to circumscribe their movements. I called the officer of my guard, and ordered him to expel the intruders; but he was so intimidated by the words of the sepoy that he was afraid to do anything.

In the morning, another sepoy appeared, saying that he had been sent by Schaykh Sahab, with instructions to me to give up the kitchen, and in no way to disturb the nabob's servants. I told him that I was not accustomed to receive such communications, and that if it were true that he came from Schaykh Sahab, he must, of course, be furnished with a letter, and that, as long as this form was not adopted, I should pay no attention to what he said. He then required a written answer from me, which I refused, not having received a written communication. However, as all my people seemed very much alarmed, and unwilling to exert themselves, I gave up the kitchen, and ordered my horses into the street. I then wrote to Schayk Sahab, requesting to know whether he was acquainted with the affronts that had been offered me: that my people were obliged to sleep in the boats, that my kitchen utensils were lying in the yard, and my horses standing in the street, that a sepoy had come in the evening, and another on the following morning, that both gave very great annoyance, and that neither his officers nor munschis afforded me any assistance. I added that I could not believe that he was cognizant of such proceedings; and as I was very sure that the sepoy acted without directions, I required that he should be punished.

I entrusted this letter to my indolent munschi, with instructions to deliver it himself into the hands of the governor. Before the letter went, Chuni Lahl arrived, learned what had occurred, and immediately went off, not to inform the governor, but to commune with his friend

Mackermal; and both soon afterwards presented themselves before me. Mackermal had met my munschi with the letter, and now a different mode of proceeding was adopted. The court-wal (the police of the city) were brought to clear the house of the intruders, and to bring everything belonging to me within the walls.

I asked for my letter, and was told that Mackermal had it. This exasperated me, and I immediately ordered my munschi to be called. He came, and on being asked for the letter, said that Mackermal had taken it. I insisted upon the letter being produced; Mackermal refused, and persisted in his refusal, though I repeated the demand three times. I at length declared that I would write another letter to Schaykh Sahab. Upon this he thought it better to give up the letter. He did so, but in order to conceal its having been opened, he handed it to my munschi, hoping that he might find some means of persuading me that the letter had not been opened, or that it had occurred by chance. I saw that the letter had been opened, but yet could not make a positive assertion of the fact. My other munschi, the son of Ramparshal, to whom the letter had been confided, and to whom it was now handed, saw the thing more plainly, and fearing that either he or his father might incur blame, said to me, that the letter had been opened. I desired that it should be handed to me, and saw clearly that treachery had been practised. I demanded of Ramparshal how this had happened, and he acknowledged that Mackermal had done it, and this excellent person tried to excuse himself by saying that his object had been to discover the name of the sepoy who had acted so badly.

CHAPTER V.

Schaykh Sahab's answer—Incomprehensible epistle—A new Munschi — Explanation from the Governor—Abstraction of my papers—Some account of Gulam Muhyiddin — Runjeet Singh's proceedings towards him—Former times in Kashmir—Jehanghir and Nur Jehan—Kapar Rahm—His history—Contrast between the former and present inhabitants of Kashmir—Condition of the artisan — Complicated system of arithmetic.

NOTWITHSTANDING Mackermal's apologies, I sent the letter of my munschi to Schaykh Sahab, and Chuni Lahl appeared in the evening with a letter, that contained neither an answer to my questions, nor any explanation of what had occurred. It was couched in these terms:

"I have received the sahab's friendly letter,

and this has been to me the occasion of great joy, though I cannot do all that friendship requires in consequence of what has occurred in Lahore. Had this not been the case, I should have been much in your society and found amusement with Ab. And Ab makes this friendship now firm, and so in future shall Ab write me letters of this kind, and I shall rejoice in them."

This letter was perfectly unintelligible. The writing was different from that of all the other communications I had received from the governor. I could make nothing of it. I told Chuni Lahl that I was astonished at receiving such a letter, and did not know what to think.

About this time I found myself in want of a skilful penman, and though I had three scriveners in my service, I wished for one still more expert to pen some letters that I wished to have written. I had scarcely expressed the wish, when it was fulfilled. An old man presented himself, who seemed to possess the capabilities I required. I liked him, and an engagement was soon made. It happens in India, in some cases at least, that one comes more directly to the point in question than in Europe. The conversation turned upon the late events in my establishment, and my new munschi declared it to be his opinion that Schaykh Sahab was wholly ignorant of the entire transaction, which he believed to be the result of Mackermal's intrigues. He advised me to send one of my own munschis to the governor, with an oral message. This proposition pleased me, and I sent my eldest munschi, that is, he who was longest in my service, to Schaykh Sahab the following morning, with a detailed account of all that had occurred. The munschi returned in about two hours, bearing a message from the governor, couched in the sweetest words, assuring me that he had not been applied to, during the proceedings that had given me so much annoyance. He concluded with the warmest protestations of friendship, entreating me to command his services in any way I needed. He had ordered the two offending sepoys to be imprisoned, and at my request promised not to send Mackermal or Uttumjin to me again. He also laid a solemn injunction on my munschi to let him know everything I needed, and that there should be no mistake in this respect, he said that he would, every day, send one of his own khitmatgars to learn my wishes, and to see that his orders had been fulfilled. More than this I could not desire; as I looked upon such an arrangement as a protection against the recurrence of such vexations as I had lately suffered.

Notwithstanding the efforts of the governor to prevent all communication between me and persons who had cause to complain of him, notwithstanding that he surrounded me with his own creatures, some of the aggrieved still found their way to me, entreating that I would interfere for the restoration of their rights. Though unwilling to meddle in business that did not directly concern me, I could not always refuse the petitioners.

In order to make the position of my clients better understood, I had intended to give some account of the life of Gulam Muhyiddin; but on looking over my papers after the lapse of several years, I find many leaves have been abstracted from my journal. That there was a definite object in the abstraction of these papers, there can be no doubt, for these were precisely the pages that contained incidents from the life of Gulam Muhyiddin and Gulab Singh, which it is probable these gentlemen would not wish to have brought to light. The journal was, after the Indian fashion, enclosed in a wrapper with a string, and it was very easy to steal away some of the leaves without exciting suspicion on my part.

These pages, as I have said, contained some of the principal events of the life of Gulam Muhyiddin and Gulab Singh. Amongst other things, there was an account of their perfidious, and, in many respects, dishonourable conduct towards the old Rajah of Iskadu, as well as towards many others. I had also noted down all the particulars I learned concerning Iskadu and Ladak, with an account of Gulab Singh's unsuccessful campaign against Gilgit and the Chinese territories, and many particulars of the conquest of Kashmir by the Sikhs, with exact data of the state of the shawl manufacture in Kashmir. I have not the slightest doubt that these papers were stolen by a creature of Gulab Singh's. But, it may be asked, how could a stranger, ignorant of the language in which I wrote, know the exact pages that contained an account of Gulab Singh? Nothing could be easier to a person who enjoyed freedom of access to my apartments, for as I wrote down, almost every evening a narrative of the day's proceedings, or made notes of the subjects that had been started in conversation, it was not difficult for those about me to know what I was writing, as I was often obliged to inquire the names of persons and places, which was, of course, sufficient indication of the subject about which I was employed. I was much inclined to suspect a young munschi, whom I had hired in the mountain region, and who afterwards suddenly disappeared from my suite, as we were on the borders of Gulab Singh's dominions.

Gulab Singh may congratulate himself on the possession of my papers, and I only wish that he were able to read them; but his trickery shall not avail him, for I will record all I know of his evil deeds.

I will now return to the subject that I interrupted to offer this explanation. I mentioned that many persons asked me to interfere, in their behalf, with the governor, Schaykh Sahab. Amongst these was Ahed Schah. In order to make the reader fully acquainted with the circumstances of the case, it will be necessary to mention a few of the leading traits of Gulam Muhyiddin's character.

Gulam Muhyiddin, who was of humble birth, came to Kashmir, in quality of chief munschi to the governor Moti Kham, if I remember correctly. Some reports, circulated about him, attracted the attention of Runjeet Singh, and at the time that he dismissed Moti Kham from his office of governor, he summoned Gulam Muhyiddin to an account, and fined him a considerable sum. After urging many objections and enumerating great difficulties, he produced part of the sum required, protesting that he did not possess any more, but Runjeet Singh was not to be turned from his purpose, and as Muhyiddin was endowed with an almost equal degree of perseverance, sterner means were resorted to. Runjeet Singh ordered him to be pinched with red hot irons, which process had the effect of inducing him to produce several lacs of rupees, completing the sum of fourteen lacs that had been originally demanded of him. After this Runjeet allowed him to depart, because he repeatedly swore that he did not possess another ana, and was actually reduced to beggary.

Some time after Muhyiddin's liberation, Runjeet was informed that he still possessed a great deal of gold, which was hidden in his father's tomb. This tomb was erected in the interior of Muhyiddin's house, ostensibly to honour his father's memory, but in reality, to conceal his treasures, and here the pious son was to be seen daily offering up his prayers. The tomb was opened and found to contain, not a mouldering skeleton, but solid gold. Of the sincerity with which he offered up prayers at that shrine, there could be no doubt. Runjeet not only took the gold that was in the tomb, but ordering the house to be carefully searched, discovered a great deal more, which he also appropriated to his own use.

There are to be seen in India, bars of pure

gold, smelted into a solid mass, and to which the Indians give a name that might very well be translated "gold bricks." Under the floor of Muhyiddin's private room was found a flooring of these gold bricks, the walls were filled with them, the beams of the roof were hollowed out and stuffed with the same precious material. Runjeet Singh took all this, and, including a lac of rupees that Gulab Singh paid for Muhyiddin's liberation it is said, that by the entire transaction he gained thirty lacs of rupees.

Affairs had now taken a very bad turn for Muhyiddin. He and his son were necessitated to become munschis at a monthly pay of about eight or ten rupees each. Both supported themselves in this manner for some time. Runjeet Singh died, and under Karak Singh's government, Muhyiddin throve better. He was made governor of Kashmir, and Gulab Singh gave him a lac of rupees. It is said that the physical weakness from which Muhyiddin suffers, is in consequence of the tortures to which Runjeet Singh subjected him when he forced him to yield his gold; but whatever he lost at that time, he has since fully indemnified himself.

This is the man under whose iniquitous rule Kashmir now groans—unhappy Kashmir, which seems destined to feel for a long time the tyrant's rod! This country, so richly endowed by nature with everything that could render its inhabitants happy, is plunged in the deepest misery. Its people say, that in former times, under its Hindoo rulers, the state of things was different; but how far this is true it would be difficult to judge. Modern history tells us of the festive scenes of which Kashmir was the theatre in the time of Jehanghir and his beloved Nur Jehan, who made a yearly visit of some months to Kashmir, where they passed their time in festivities of every kind; and here, in the voluptuous summer nights, the lake reflected brilliant illuminations and fantastic fireworks, and the air re-echoed to the sound of song and dance. The reign of Ackbar, the first of the Moguls who possessed Kashmir, leaves no record of merry days passed in the happy valley; this conquest was too newly gained to be enjoyed in peace.

After the reigns of Ackbar and Jehanghir, the first intelligence we receive of Kashmir is from Bernier, who visited the happy valley in the suite of Aurungzib. A dependant province, far removed from the seat of government, will occupy little of the historian's attention, and the details that we receive of its history are generally due to an interest awakened in the breast of a private individual. This has been the fate of Kashmir; and whether the people of the land suffered less or enjoyed more under one Aghan or Sikh governor than another, does not alter the general aspect of the history of the country, which presents an unbroken chain of oppression, disasters and misery.

The Sikh governor who enjoys the best reputation amongst the inhabitants of Kashmir is Kapar Rham. The term of his viceroyalty is compared by the people of the valley, to those pleasant days when Jehanghir used to make an annual visit there. Kapar Rham remitted to the government every year forty-two lacs of rupees, and the country was at that time happy, in comparison to what it now is; and yet for many years after the rule of Kapar Rham, the tribute amounted to only twenty lacs, and at the present time Gulam Muhyiddin returns but six lacs of rupees yearly, while the country, so far from being benefited by the decrease in the tribute, is become still more wretched.

The mention of Kapar Rham gives me an opportunity of recording Runjeet Singh's unworthy conduct towards him. Kapar Rham was descended in the fourth degree from the excellent Dewan Mahdum Chund, (Muckum Chund), whom Runjeet hated through jealousy, and whom, in consequence, he always sent on the most dangerous expeditions, from which Muckum always returned triumphant. Runjeet Singh demanded from Kapar Rham an extra payment of some lacs of rupees, and summoned him for the fulfilment of this demand to the confines of his mountain territories, where he then was. Kapar answered that he would pay the money when it should be due, and then only what could be lawfully demanded. Runjeet asked him whether he had no money. "Yes," answered Kapar; "but I will give you only what is due to you." "Very well," said Runjeet, "we will settle our accounts."

They proceeded to do so, and meanwhile the army set out for Lahore. Upon arriving there, and the accounts being closed, it was found that Kapar had paid twelve lacs of rupees more than he really owed. Runjeet demanded three lacs more, Kapar refused, and was tortured with red-hot iron by command of the tyrant. He still persisted in his refusal, upon which his property was openly plundered. He lost fifteen lacs, partly in money partly in shawls. He was now set at liberty, with permission to return and resume the government of the province of Kashmir, but he refused; and after bestowing a lac of rupees in public charity at Amrit Sir, he retired to Hardwar, where it is said that by command of Runjeet Singh he received daily a hundred rupees. This I think very improbable, nor do I think that Kapar would have accepted a gift from Runjeet Singh. That he received valuable presents from different parts of India, particularly from the

Punjab, is certain. It is well known, and I find it recorded in my journal, that Kapar even gave away his wives.

That the present inhabitants of Kashmir are not happy is quite certain, but whether their predecessors were happy in the time when, besides a tribute of forty-two lacs of rupees, they maintained the expensive household of the pleasure-loving Kapar Rham, is a question that may be better answered by the artizan and peasant of those times than by the merchants, munschis, priests, and military officers, who were precisely those who would be likely to benefit by the luxurious expenditure of Kapar, and who would not hesitate to pronounce the country happy because they were amused. It appears to me that the happiness of the inhabitants of Kashmir has kept pace with their independence. A sneaking, slavish race of citizens is an unerring proof of the degradation of a country; whilst the open, frank demeanour, the determined and sometimes bold deportment of the honest burgher, is a clear evidence of the well-being of the land. The ancient inhabitants of Kashmir are represented as a brave and warlike race, who after they had been defeated in the valley, retired to the mountains, where they still continued the warfare, nor did they yield, until, after making the greatest sacrifices, they were overpowered by numbers.

The conviction that the people could not be kept long under the yoke, unless this unbending heroic spirit was broken, seems to have been the reason why the men were condemned to wear the female costume. This appears to have been one of the methods used to tame their fiery spirit, and humble their haughty hearts. An attempt of this kind, as may be supposed, induced many a bitter contest; and not unfrequently was the female robe torn asunder, and wrapped about the arm, made to serve as a shield. And so it passed on from generation to generation, until at length, as many believe, the feminine garb infused into the wearer a womanly spirit, and the brave Kashmerian was, at last, lost in the folds of the petticoat.

The system of peculation practised in Kashmir is more extensive than any I ever witnessed elsewhere, and could only be understood by those skilled in the arithmetical calculations of the country. The public accounts are exclusively in the hands of the Pandits, a caste as closely united as it is possible to conceive human beings can be. The Pandits, who are skilled in making the most complicated arithmetical calculations, have, from generation to generation, been intrusted with these important duties. When the Affghans in 1752 became masters of Kashmir, they, being Hindoos, did not wish to employ the Pandits, and installed their own countrymen in these offices, but the new-comers were incompetent to the task assigned them, and the Pandits were recalled. When the Sikhs conquered the Affghans, the Pandits were again dismissed, and their places given to munschis brought from the Punjab; but as the financial system of the country was not changed, these strangers were unable to arrange the accounts, and the Pandits were again recalled. The system of calculation is in itself complicated; and when it is considered that almost every individual in the country has a debtor and credit account with the government which, however perplexing, is generally made to turn to the advantage of the rulers; and when we add to this the number of government agents that are to be paid, we shall find very little difficulty in believing that the "happy valley" contains a very unhappy population.

To give a more distinct view of the state of these people, I will add a few remarks upon the system of taxation as regards each class of society. I shall begin with the tiller of the land as the foundation-stone of the social edifice. I have made calculations, which it would be wearisome to introduce here, by which I find that the tiller of the soil pays in taxes the *sixth part* of the produce of the land; and as these imposts are taken *in kind*, he has the additional expense of supplying the seed.

The coolies and bearers who accompanied me from Kashmir to Lahore gave me the following account of their position. "When we return to Kashmir," said they, "as it will be well known that we shall each have received six rupees, there will be sent into our houses by order of the governor, for each man, two measures of maize. The price of one measure in the bazaar is only eight anas, but we shall be charged two rupees, so that all we shall have earned will pass into the governor's hands."

The artizans and weavers of shawls are in an equally miserable condition. The daily wages of each is four anas, of which he must pay two to the governor; and for the two remaining anas, singara, a kind of vegetable, is sent into his house, and, I need scarcely mention, at the same rate at which it is sold to the coolies. This singara is the cheapest of all kinds of food, and were it not so abundant, it would not be possible for a large portion of the inhabitants of Kashmir to live on the slender pittance allowed by the governor. The singara, which is a kind of marine-vegetable, is found in abundance in the lakes; and yet this food, which is so bounteously supplied by nature, is subjected to a tax taken *in kind*, and which forms a stock afterwards sold out at an exorbitant price. The lakes supply another kind of food in the lotus-seed, which is not unlike the singara.

If my readers are not already convinced that the oppression under which the inhabitants of

Kashmir labour exceeds comparison, I will lead them into the interior of the workman's dwelling and present a more detailed picture of his misery.

I have already said that a good workman—a weaver, for instance—earns four anas per day, half of which goes to the governor, and the remainder is expended in the pūrchase of provisions. It is evident that the poverty of the family must be extreme, for which reason the children are set to work almost as soon as they are able to use their limbs. The son, at five years of age, enters on the business of weaving, and his wages are proportioned to his baby exertions. As he advances in growth and skill, his pay is raised, subject to the usual taxation; and thus another human being enters on a career of wretchedness, and rears children, who in turn, become heirs to his misery.

As one object in this system is never to allow the workman ready money, the government provides clothes, firing, and the other household necessaries, charging as usual, a hundred per cent profit. This is managed very skilfully, and so arranged that the poor artizan is always in debt; and I will add, that the shawl weavers seem to be the most unfortunate.

The arithmetical calculations in a system like this must be very complicated, and could only be made by persons intimately acquainted with the details. It is for this reason that the Pandits, who have been in this employment, from generation to generation for centuries, still retain it. This class is certainly the most happy in the land. They live in sage retirement, and from the highest to the lowest are bound together in such close connection, that no governor has yet been able to shake their influence.

The profit arising to the government, or to speak more correctly, to the governor of Kashmir, from the manufacture of shawls, is enormous. Besides the two anas paid by each workman out of his wages, there is a tax of twenty-five rupees on each shawl. And when we consider the manner in which these poor people are taxed, and provisions sold to them, I have no hesitation in saying, that two shawls sold for some hundreds, do not cost the seller more than a few rupees worth of singara. It may be asked why do not all who can afford to employ workmen, get shawls made. The number of workmen is not great, and nearly all are employed by government. I say nearly all, for there are a few private individuals in Kashmir, who employ shawl weavers. These employers are Affghans and Bengalese, though I think it very probable that the latter are only the nominees of some rich Kashmerian Pandits. The shawls manufactured for these persons are taxed in the same manner as those woven for the government, with the exception of the two anas, taken from the workman's wages.

The number of weavers employed by private individuals is very small, nor would the governor be much pleased to see others interfere with his profits. General Ventura once traded in these shawls, and had great numbers woven here; but as he never came himself to Kashmir, and as these goods must have passed through the hands of intermediate persons, he may not have derived great profit from the traffic. He afterwards got shawls woven at Amrit Sir.

I may in another page, say a little more

about the manufacture of shawls, but I will now turn to speak of the position of the soldiers. These are scarcely better off than the other classes of which I have spoken. A regular receipt of pay is not to be thought of, nor indeed, strictly speaking, do they receive pay at all. The pay is always in arrear, and the accounts are so managed, that the soldiers are always made to appear in debt. The sepoys who accompanied me from Kashmir were very communicative. They said that in consequence of my express wish on the subject, the governor had paid them on setting out. Each had received six rupees as a compensation for six month's service, and he was obliged to be content, for according to the arrangement of the accounts they were made to appear in debt to the government. Once as the army was marching against the Chinese, Gulab Singh ordered that each soldier should receive a present of one lohy and one rupee, but when the campaign was finished, the gift was set down as a debt. This mode of annulling presents was by no means unusual.

The old munschi, whom I have already

mentioned, and who became every day more attached to me, was the pearl of munschis. Not only was he a skilful penman, but he had distinguished himself by the composition of several satirical poems full of wit and spirit. The subjects of these compositions were matters of local interest. I was as much pleased with his personal qualities as with his conversation. He was more candid and fearless in his remarks than any Oriental I had ever met. He was not a native of Kashmir, nor did he intend to abide there permanently. He spoke freely about the state of the country, and as his observations were very judicious, I noted down some of them.

CHAPTER VI.

Account given by the old Munschi—Condition of the agriculturist in Kashmir—Sepoys and Munschis—Difficulty of presenting a petition to the Governor—A letter from the Schaykh Sahab—Some account of Gulab Singh and his family — His expedition against Chinese Tartary—The Rajah of Iskardu—Mohamed Shah.

"The government," said my munschi, "is, with respect to the people, worse than anybody's fancy could portray. A zemindar, who wishes to rent and cultivate a tract of land, is never refused permission to do so. All that is required of him, is to subscribe to the ordinary conditions, that is, he must give three fourths of the revenue of the farm to the government.

Even the remaining fourth is not wholly his own. It is taxed in various ways. The seed for the ground is supplied by government; but at usurious prices, so that the position of the zemindar is most distressing."

I shall here take an opportunity of speaking of the denominations of the different classes in India. All those who are neither landholders, nor merchants, artizans, labourers, nor bearers, are divided into two classes—munschis and sepoys. The latter wear a sword, the former carry in the hand a kulumdan, or little roll of paper. Every man wishes for some mark of distinction; many a munschi, who wishes to play the part of the great man, carries a sword, and the khansama decorates himself with a kalumdan. Every man, whose office entitles him to wear a sword, is in the sepoy class, and all those employed in keeping the accounts of government, transcribing, translating, &c., are munschis, and are esteemed according to the pay they receive. The sepoys and munschis are the two arms by which the government rule, and they in turn are supported by the country.

My munschi having described the position of

the zemindars, proceeded: "It is still worse with others who stand in immediate connection with the government, especially those who venture to enter the divan. In the first place, it is very difficult to pass the outer gate, where any one who has not an especial recommendation, is received with blows and all sorts of ill-treatment. Should he overcome these impediments, he may, after encountering numerous difficulties, pass through the many doors that still lie in his way, until he reaches the hall of audience. Here he leaves his shoes at the threshold, and advances into the divan. Should he be so fortunate as to return, he no longer finds any trace of his shoes. They have disappeared. There is no remedy, and he walks on, until he reaches the outer gate. Here he meets a ferasch, to whom he bewails his loss, and describes the impossibility of going to his boat without shoes. Upon this, the ferasch offers to lend him a pair, for which accomodation he charges the moderate sum of one, sometimes two rupees. The shoes are returned to the ferasch when the borrower arrives at his boat. So that, you see," said my informant, "no sensible man will be anxious to enter the divan."

"If it sometimes happens that a man gets into arrears with the government and cannot pay his debts, no further questions are asked, the debtor is not imprisoned; but the wealthy members of his family are seized, and obliged to pay. Should he have no immediate relatives, his neighbours and friends are held accountable, and to establish the bond of friendship in this case, it is quite sufficient that a man has been heard to wish the hapless debtor 'good morning' as he passed along the street; the luckless acquaintance is declared to be an intimate friend, and involved in all the terrible consequences that a Kashmerian entails upon his friends in such a case."

This account given by the munschi corresponds with all that I had previously heard. I should never finish, were I to relate all the trickeries practised in this country. Still some are so entertaining that they are worth relating: others are so nefarious, that they ought to be exposed. The office of door-keeper at the palace, is, as is well known, a post of much importance in Eastern nations. This situation was filled in Kashmir by the uncle of the governor, a man who like his nephew, had risen from the dregs of the people, and whose sympathy with that worthy relative, arose more from a similarity of character, than the ties of blood. If any one has a petition to present, or a request to prefer to the governor, he must, according to established rule, first try to pass through the gate-way. The passage must be purchased, and the toll paid must, in this case, be proportioned to the dignity of the official, who being uncle to the governor, cannot be treated as an ordinary person. A confidential servant, with several sepoys, stands at the gate. The good-will of these worthies is purchased, and the petitioner is conducted into the presence of the governor's uncle. To this gentleman, a very considerable offering is made, for which he promises to procure the supplicant an audience. An understanding exists between the uncle and nephew as to the division of the spoil.

Everything being arranged between the door-keeper and his *protégé*, the latter is conducted by his patron to the threshold of the hall of audience. Here the power of the door-keeper ceases, but not the influence of the uncle, whose relationship with the governor allows him greater privileges. In the East a fool is treated with particular indulgence, and the uncle of the governor assumes the character on this occasion, that he may play his part with greater licence. If the purchase money given by the petititioner has fully satisfied his wishes, he takes his *protégé* by the hand, leads him into the hall, and conducts him directly to the governor, requesting that he will listen to his *protégé's* petition, saying that he is a good man, and that the Schaykh Sahab must do him justice. All this, be it understood, is uttered with an affectation of foolery. The schaykh replies: "What do you wish! let it be! let it be! I will hear the man, as well as all the others." The uncle is not repulsed, he becomes more pressing, and as he and his nephew understand each other perfectly well, the success of the petitioner depends on the money that has been paid. Of the money obtained in this way, the uncle receives only a share, the larger portion is pocketed by the governor.

The Schaykh Sahab had learned that I wished to buy either a Turkish or Affghan horse, and wrote me the following letter on this subject.

"I have sought for horses for you in every direction, and, with great difficulty, have found one. It belongs to a merchant, who is himself very fond of horses, and has been several times offered a large price for this animal. I have abated the tax of fifty rupees, and fixed the price of the horse at four hundred. For this sum you can have but a welaid, or native horse. It is only through friendship that the merchant consents to dispose of his horse at this price. I send the animal that you may see it."

Speaking of persons whose character for honesty rests upon a very bad foundation, naturally brings Gulab Singh to my recollection. The family consists of Gulab and his two brothers, Dehan and Sutjed Singh. Another brother, whose name I have forgotten, died. There are, besides a son of Gulab Singh, called Mia Singh, and two sons of Dehan's, Hera and Mia Singh. To Europeans, this family has been generally known by the name of the Jumbu. This appellation must be of a modern date, as it was under Runjeet Singh that Gulab wormed himself, by the most unworthy means, into the governorship of Jumbu. The entire family pursued their interest conjointly, the object of which was to secure to themselves the sovereignty of the mountain regions, within the Sutlej and Indus. Sutjed seemed, in some degree, to deviate from the general aim of the family. In the late catastrophe at Lahore Dehan Singh was, as I have mentioned, murdered, in consequence of which, Gulab became the head of the family.

Gulab Singh and his brothers were Radjputs from the mountains, and, in the commencement of their career, held very subordinate situations. Gulab and his elder brother entered the service of Runjeet Singh as sepoys. It happened that once during a campaign, the brother was placed as sentinel outside Runjeet's tent. The latter, who had an eye for personal beauty, was pleased with the soldierly appearance of the Radjput, and promoted him, giving him a place about his person. The advancement of one brother was a stepping-stone for the others. Gulab and Dehan Singh shared their brother's good fortune, and in a short time, Dehan enjoyed the special favour of the rajah.

The influence of the Radjput increased daily, the elder brother died, and Dehan Singh was soon advanced to the dignity of prime minister. Gulab Singh remained in high favour at the court, and enjoyed an important military post. It was in this position that he made his first great step. He triumphed over his hereditary liege, the Rajah of Jumbu, and installed himself in his place.

Gulab Singh quarrelled with the Rajah of Jumbu, and remained three years with the Rajah of Kischtewar. At the end of this time he learned that Runjeet Singh intended to send an expedition against Jumbu, and immediately offered his services. Runjeet put him at the head of a body of troops, and Gulab took possession of Jumbu. He now wrote to the Rajah of Kischtewar, saying that Runjeet was about to send an army against him, and advising him to prepare for his defence.

The rajah followed his advice, and wrote to tell him so. Upon this, Gulab Singh forged letters addressed to Runjeet Singh. These letters were written in the name of some of the chief persons in Kischtewar, inviting Runjeet to come there. Gulab wrote to the rajah, enclosing these letters, and told him that it was now useless to think of resistance, as his own people were opposed to him. At the same time, he advised him to punish the delinquents. The rajah ordered his vizier to be cut down. The attempt failed, the vizier was only wounded, but he was thrown into prison. The vizier made such earnest protestations of his innocence, that the rajah hesitated, and wrote to Gulab for further advice.

The latter told him that he was betrayed, that it would be better to get the vizier executed, and come himself to Jumbu. The poor rajah did so; his treacherous enemy seized and threw him into prison, and without opposition took possession of Kischtewar. He now wrote to Runjeet Singh, telling him of his success, and of the great things he had done for him. Runjeet invested him with the governorship of the district, upon which the former rajah was set at liberty. He set out for Lahore, and appealed for justice to Runjeet Singh. As many sirdars interested themselves in his favour, it is probable that something would have been done for him, had not Gulab Singh bribed his servants, who, for a sum of ten thousand rupees, poisoned him.

Gulab Singh relaxed nothing of the activity with which he had commenced his career. He constantly endeavoured to extend his rule through the mountain region. His efforts were powerfully aided by Dehan Singh. In 1838, Gulab projected an expedition against Little Thibet. As the troops were embarking, a boat, containing ninety men, was overturned, and all in it drowned. This was considered a bad omen, and the expedition was abandoned. But Gulab Singh may be looked upon as sole master of Kashmir, that his tax-collectors and officers are to be found even in Salamabad.

It is said that Gulab Singh, having suppressed a revolt in one of the provinces, ordered the prisoners to be flayed alive before his eyes. One of the executioners of this cruel order, showing some symptoms of mercy or remorse, Gulab called out to him, and asked whether it was his father or mother that was under his hands, that he seemed so faint-hearted. Of the human skins obtained in this manner, Gulab Singh ordered two to be stuffed with straw, and the hands bound together in a supplicating attitude. The heads, having been cut off, were fixed in an inverted position on the stuffed trunks. These figures were placed on either side of the way, Gulab Singh wishing by this example to give his son a lesson in the art of cruelty.

I have already said that Gulab Singh had fixed his eyes upon the mountain district between the Sutlej and the Indus. Having extended his power over the portion that lay nearest to him, he wished to advance further. To Little Thibet he turned that sort of loving gaze with which the cat ogles the mouse in the trap. He made an attempt, succeeded, and took possession of Ladak. This conquest encouraged him to think of Chinese Tartary. He ordered his troops to assemble from every quarter, as he intended to cross the Chinese frontiers. In this expedition he met with a signal defeat. I had a conversation with a sepoy, who had been, at that time, in the service of Gulab Singh. He told me, in his fashion, that the Chinese are a very strange kind of people. It is their custom to forgive the first and second offence, but a third is punished very seriously. This principle is carried out, not only in civil, but in military affairs. When the Sikh army approached they saw a Chinese force ready to receive them, as they thought. They were, however, very much surprised to see the enemy retire as they advanced. Encouraged by this, they went on more boldly, and were soon in sight of a second army of Chinese, which like the first retreated before them. A little further on, a third army awaited them, which they hoped to put to flight as easily as the others. But in this they were sadly disappointed. The new army did not fly from their attack; the soldiers resisted boldly, and it was now the turn of the Sikhs to fly. The slaughter was tremendous, and their leader, Zurawak Singh, was amongst the slain. Still worse did the Sikhs fare at Gilghit, where, besides being routed and numbers slain, the survivors suffered all the horrors of famine.

Gulab Singh was more successful in Iskardu than he had been in Chinese Tartary; but it was by treachery that he conquered. Ahmed Shah was rajah of the place. He governed with justice, and was beloved and respected by his subjects. He had many sons, the eldest of whom, Mohamed Shah, had been appointed his successor. This young man governed in the district of Hasara. It was found that he abused his authority, upon which his father deprived him of his post, which he bestowed upon another son, Mohamed Ali Khan. The eldest son, enraged at this, left Iskardu, and crossing the frontiers, retired into the nearest Sikh fort, and placed himself under the protection of the garrison.

Gulab Singh was delighted when he heard of this, and sent to Mohamed Shah, promising to make him Rajah of Iskardu. When everything was arranged between them, an army was equipped and led to Iskardu by Mohamed, who knew all the passes of the land. Ahmed Shah was taken prisoner and sent to Jumbu, where he still draws on a life of misery. Mohamed is only a puppet in the hands of the Sikhs; for though he enjoys the title of rajah, Gulab Singh is the real sovereign of the country. Mohamed Shah finds but too late that he has betrayed his family and his country, without attaining the object of his guilty ambition.

CHAPTER VII.

My mode of life in Kashmir—My acquaintances and companions—Kashmerian imports—Paschm—Tea—Different modes of preparing tea—Choob-chini—Regimen followed by patients whilst using it—Shawls of Kashmir—Persons employed in the manufacture of shawls—Washing the shawls—Trade with France—Misery of the weavers—Attachment of the Kashmerians to their country.

MY manner of living in Kashmir had now assumed a uniformity, that was a natural consequence of my long residence in the country. I confined myself to the town. The poor people's backs had suffered so much in dragging my luggage, that I had become weary of making excursions. Besides, I knew that in leaving Kashmir I should have a view of that part of the valley that I had not yet seen.

I passed some hours of the morning in my private occupations: in the afternoon I strolled abroad, and the evening was passed in the society of a few persons with whom I had become acquainted in Kashmir. Amongst these, the literary munschi of whom I have already spoken, held a conspicuous place. He sometimes entertained us with a recital of some of his satirical poems, in which Kashmir was described in colours very different from those in which Paradise is generally painted. Another of my visitors was a Pandit, well versed in Sanscrit, who read to us passages, sometimes from the Veddas, sometimes from the Ramayana, which he explained in Hindoo. Ahed Schah, for whom I had conceived a great affection, never failed to come, and Mirza Ahmed was also one of our intimates. He was the commissioned agent of the government for the shawl manufacture. He also transacted business for Gulam Muhyiddin and for General Ventura. The post that he held obliged him to travel a great deal. He had been frequently in Thibet, and was acquainted with every inch of the valley of Kashmir and the surrounding country. He possessed an extensive knowledge of business, and having been lately appointed vakil by the English government, he was ready upon all occasions to aid Europeans with his advice and services.

Amongst the countries, from which imports arrive in Kashmir, are Thibet, Ladak, and Iskardu. Besides paschm, the goats' hair of which the shawls are made, and which may be called the sinews of the land, tea is also imported. This celebrated plant is here called "tschay." That brought from China is of two kinds. One, which is coarse, is made up in packages of four or five pounds, sown in a red leather cover. Small pieces of stick are sometimes found mixed in this kind of tea. Though coarse in appearance, the flavour is good; but this tea is far inferior to another kind that is used here, and which is brought from Thibet. This is not packed so tightly as the other; the packages are sown, but the tea is not more tightly pressed than we are accustomed to see it in Europe. The packages are brought from Thibet by sheep, goats, or men; I have never seen horses employed as carriers of this article.

With the inhabitants of Kashmir, as well as with those of Thibet, tea is an article of daily use. It is to be seen at every meal. The manner of preparing it in the East has been many times described. Few travellers from other countries have passed here, who have not dedicated some pages of their journal to the history of tea in its native soil. This must be my apology for saying a few words on the subject. In Kashmir, tea is prepared in two ways. The one is called sweet tea, the other salt. There is another manner of preparing this favourite beverage, which, though not so generally practised here, is said to be the Chinese mode.

The sweet tea is simply a decoction as in Europe: to this is added cinnamon, or cinnamon flowers and sugar, but no milk. There is also put in a little soda, which is here called bussa, and which is brought from Thibet. The soda is said to draw the tea more quickly; it also improves the colour. This tea is seldom used at meals; the salt tea is preferred at such times.

The salt tea is prepared in the same manner as the sweet, but instead of cinnamon and sugar, salt and milk are added. Cream is considered a great improvement. The tea prepared in this manner is something like soup, and though not so savoury as what is called the sweet tea, it is more nutritious. I have heard that in Thibet the tea-leaves are used as a vegetable. I felt a curiosity to taste this dish, and ordered it whilst in Kashmir. I must confess that it was very palatable; but what is not made savoury in India, where the cooks are so well skilled in the art of spicing, that the original taste of the viand is lost? A man could eat anything dressed in their fashion, that was not so tough as to pull out his teeth.

The natives of Kashmir and Thibet never travel without their tea equipage. Every man carries his little copper can slung at his saddle-bow, and all the accessories in his pocket. This little can, or tea-kettle, is about twelve or fourteen inches high, and two-and-a-half in diameter. It is furnished with a handle and spout, and bears a strong resemblance to the oil-pitcher of the ancient Greeks.

Choob-chini is a vegetable production scarcely less esteemed in these countries than tea. It is a universal medicine, but particularly esteemed as a purifier of the blood. The manner in which this medicine is used betrays something of the fantastic spirit of the "Morning Land."

The patient who wishes to try the efficacy of the choob-chini, must drink a decoction of the root for at least forty days. During this time he must abstain from all business. The house, or at least the chamber, in which he abides, must be furnished afresh: new servants must be hired, and everything calculated to awaken old impressions should be banished. His ears are to be delighted with the sounds of the sweetest music, and his eyes amused by the efforts of the most graceful dancers. All about him must be gay. Nothing is to be mentioned before him that could cause him the slightest annoyance, none of the cares that bind him to the outer world are to be named in his presence.

This regimen naturally involves a good deal of expense, so that choob-chini is a luxury reserved for the rich.

There are few countries to which nature has been more bountiful than to Kashmir. This lovely and fertile valley contains within itself abundant means of supplying the wants of its inhabitants. Surrounded by lofty mountains, the passes of which can be easily guarded, the whole country may be securely protected from invaders, whilst, for internal intercourse, every facility is afforded by the lakes and rivers, covered with innumerable boats.

Heron feathers are much admired in Kashmir. They are sometimes sold at a rupee each. It is forbidden to kill the birds, on which account they are watched during the time of moulting, and the feathers carefully collected. The handsomest are, of course, kept for the maha-rajah. These feathers are used as ornaments for horses as well as riders.

The shawls of Kashmir, which have been celebrated through centuries, deserve a particular notice here. I have already spoken of the weavers and their miserable condition, but as the material of which the shawls is made passes through many processes before reaching their hands, I will speak of each in succession.

To begin at the commencement, I will first speak of the paschm, or raw material. This is the hair of a goat that feeds upon the mountain pasture in Thibet. The entire fleece is not used in making the shawls, it is only the under and finer hair that is fit for this purpose. Much has been said of the effects of climate and local circumstances in producing the growth of this paschm, and it is certain that goats brought to Kashmir, and feeding in the valley or on the mountains, do not produce the paschm in the same perfection as those that feed on the Thibetian mountains. The wool or hair is of two colours, white and brown, but the former is the most prized.

I have already mentioned that the shawl trade is, almost exclusively, in the hands of the government. Though there are a few private individuals who are allowed to manufacture shawls, it is under certain restrictions. There is a large supply of paschm kept in the government stores, and this is sold to the weavers.

Women are employed to spin the paschm, which is afterwards dyed. It is strange that the green used in this operation is not manufactured in the country. It is extracted from coarse, cheap, light green cloth, of which great quantities are every year brought from England. On this account, the green dye is not good, neither is the black, but the red, blue, and yellow are beautiful.

A person of great importance in the shawl manufacturer, is the designer of the patterns. They are very few of these men in Kashmir. Their business is to invent new designs to satisfy the varying taste of the public. The sketch being made, it is handed over to a person who draws it in chalks, or Indian ink. It is then transferred to the painter, who gives to the innumerable flowers their proper hue. The duty of the reckoner then commences. This is a very troublesome occupation, and requires more than mere mechanical skill. It is necessary that the number of threads needed for each colour should be counted. The number of reckoners is almost as small as that of the designers. Their directions to the weavers are written on little billets in the following style: 1 white, 3 red, 1 yellow, 2 light blue, 2 dark blue, 1 red, &c. &c.

When the threads are fixed in the loom, a weaver begins to work at either end, so that the centre of the shawl is the part last finished. As these shawls are made in pairs, one pattern will suffice for two looms, one man reading aloud the number of threads to be employed.

On the shawls manufactured by private persons, a large tax must be paid, nor is the shawl allowed to be taken from the loom until the government officer is satisfied in this particular. The shawl is then stamped, and the owner may do with it as he pleases. The shawls must be washed, and to see these valuable articles flung carelessly on the stones on the shores of the lake by the washers, who remain standing in the water, one would not suppose that this operation required extraordinary skill; and yet, some washers enjoy a higher reputation than others. It is even said that there are parts of the lake where these lavations are better performed than in others. If such be the case, I should attribute this advantage to the peculiar qualities of the clay, which in those places esteemed best for washing, presents a different appearance from that found in other parts of the shore.

These shawls are not less an article of luxury in Kashmir than in other countries. They are more prized in Asia and even in India than in Europe. A European lady would be glad to possess one of these shawls, but persons of high rank in Kashmir and India vie with one another in striving to purchase a great number of these articles, and so enjoy the gratification of displaying a great variety, a display which must, no doubt, humble to the dust a less fortunate rival.

The shawl of Kashmir is, perhaps, the only article of apparel that improves by wear, but certain it is that one of these beautiful fabrics which has been worn for some time, and even washed, becomes brighter in colour, and more pliant to the touch than when new. One of these shawls may be worn for years without losing anything of its beauty This circumstance is the cause of great variation in the price and value of the shawl. I have said that to a certain degree, the shawls improve by wear, and even by being washed; but notwithstanding this, the new shawl is the dearest, and with many persons it is a point of vanity to wear their shawls unwashed as an incontestible proof of their newness. The shawl will through use acquire a certain flexibility, which certainly improves its appearance; it may also become soiled, and it is then necessary that it should be washed. This operation, though it adds to the beauty, lessens the value of the fabric, in which case the owner sometimes sells the shawl. Numbers of shawls which have been thus worn and washed, become again objects of traffic, and are re-sold by merchants in other countries to persons, who have not sufficient experience on such matters, to discern that their purchase is not new. I have been told that the greater number of the shawls sold in the Punjab, have been washed, and of course, the same can be said of those exported to Europe.

The maha-rajah, governors of provinces, and such persons, who feel no anxiety to convince the beholders that the shawls they wear are quite new, dress only in such as have been washed. Their vanity is at rest on this point, as it is well known that they have numbers unwashed in their stores.

Frequent washings lessen the value of the shawl; but the colours are so excellent, and so little affected by time, that connoisseurs cannot determine the age of a shawl by its appearance, even when it has been a long time in wear. In such cases, the pattern serves as a guide, for though the fabric of the Kashmir shawls has been the same through centuries, the patterns change—and fashion, through this medium, asserts her power.

During the last ten or fifteen years, a brisk trade in shawls has been carried on between France and Kashmir. This intercouse has been greatly promoted through the influence of the French gentlemen resident at Lahore. I have been told by excellent authority that the French buy shawls of inferior quality in Kashmir, which in their own country they rip up, and out of the paschm thus procured, the best French shawls are woven.

General Ventura took a very active interest in this trade, and during some years had an agent, a French gentleman, in Kashmir. He afterwards removed him to Amrit Şir, where shawls are manufactured for the General.

The French agents were in the habit of sending patterns, as well as shawls, to their own country. One of the designers here told me an anecdote on this subject, in which he seemed to take especial delight. Repeated orders had come from France for new patterns; these demands he endeavonred to satisfy, but he was still teased for "something new." At length, a model was sent him, as a sample of what was wished for; and the Kashmerian was not a little amused when he found that this pattern was a design of his own, which he had drawn many years before. "So," said the artist, "it appears there can be no better models found for us than those we have ourselves designed."

The fine brown paschm is woven into garments called djatters, which are highly prized on account of their lightness and warmth. The price varies from twenty to eighty rupees. It is said that a djatter, lined with the same material of which it is made, is sufficient protection against the most severe cold.

Sheep's wool is woven into a material called battu. This stuff is white, or silver-gray, and forms the ordinary clothing of the natives. Though not very handsome, it is very durable. There is a beautiful white paschmin stuff exported from Thibet, which is much sought for at Lahore, particularly during the winter months, the usual season for wearing mourning, when shawls, and all garments of variegated colours, are laid aside. It is said that Hera Singh possesses a large stock of robes, made of this white paschmin stuff. He had an opportunity of acquiring them through his uncle.

I have said a great deal about Kashmir: I have spoken of the beauty of the climate, and of the misery of the inhabitants, of the wondrous elegance of the fabrics manufactured there, and of the wretchedness of the artizan. Under the present government, there appears to be no hope of a better state of things, and yet the Kashmerians seem to be enamoured of affliction, or, to speak more correctly, they are so deeply attached to their native land, that the idea of emigration is, to them, insupportable. Many efforts have been made to induce them to form colonies, away from the valley in which they were born; but, rather than break that mysterious tie, that filial bond which binds them to "Fatherland," they endure oppression and injustice, they toil, and are unrepaid; but they still behold the blue sky reflected in their own unruffled lake, they inhale the balmy air, cooled and purified in its passage over the snow-topped mountains. Their oppressors cannot deprive them of these enjoyments, and they live on, slaves in their native land, unallured by the temptations held out to them to settle elsewhere.

A few shawl-weavers have been persuaded to settle down in Amrit Sir; but the general opinion is, that did things assume a milder aspect in Kashmir, they would return to the valley.

The English government made an attempt to bring some of these weavers to Ludiana, on the Sutlej. A large bazaar was built, shops and houses for the workmen were erected, and everything done that was supposed likely to please and encourage them. Paschm and wool were to be brought from Rampur, the depot of the trade with Thibet. These materials were to be given at first cost to the workmen; but, incredible as it may appear, the attempt failed. The houses and shops that had been erected at Ludiana were gradually deserted, and the Kashmerians returned to their oppressors in the valley, rejecting the milder sway of the English.

CHAPTER VIII.

Change of season—Approach of winter—Recollections of home—Letter from Hera Singh—Thoughts before setting out—Retrospective glance at Kashmir—Temple on Solimans Mountain—Horses of the country—Their skill in travelling over the mountains—Parwanah from the Maha-rajah—Farewell visit to the Governor—His professions of friendship.

My stay in Kashmir had now been of long duration. The winter was coming on. The mornings and evenings were becoming cool, and the nipping air reminded me of the autumn months in my own land, when the hoar frosts cover the plain, and when, over hill and vale, the huntsman's cry and echoing horn resound. But I was far away from those scenes of sylvan sport; and the snow-line, which descended gradually lower on the Thibetian range, announced the approach of winter under very different auspices, from those with which I had once hailed the change of season.

I was impatient to leave, and waited anxiously for letters from Lahore, before the arrival of which I could not depart. These had not yet come, but Chuni Lahl had received a letter from the Rajah Hera Singh. This letter he allowed me to read. The contents were as follows:

"Parwanah Chuni Lahl Jemida,

"I have received thy letter, and perceive by it that Sahaban intends to go to Attok and Peshawur. Considering the friendship that exists between the two governments, thou must, with sweet-tuned tongue, whisper in Sahaban's ear, that, in my opinion, it would not be safe, at the present time, to travel in the mountains, because we cannot now trust the Bunmanis, the inhabitants of the mountain jungles. Write to me on this subject."

It was evident, from this epistle, that it would be wiser to abandon my design of passing through Attok and Peshawur. Under this conviction, I turned a willing ear to Chuni Lahl's "sweet-tuned tongue," and declared that I was willing to abandon my former intention, and take the shortest way to Lahore. This was very satisfactory, but I was still obliged to delay my departure until a formal permission should arrive from Hera Singh.

During my stay in Kashmir, I had become well acquainted with the environs. Now that I was about to depart, I again cast a look on those places that I had so often visited. The ruin of the Hindoo temple at Mutten—as Abu Fazel pronounced the word—or Marten, as it is now written, was one of my favourite haunts. The situation of this temple was charming, commanding a view of the valley, and the mountains on the south and west. The temple seems to have been a massive and firmly-constructed building. It is now a heap of ruins—not even a fakir makes his abode there.

On the summit of Suliman's mountain, there is a temple, in good preservation, dedicated to the Maha Deo. The well-chosen site gives the temple a very imposing effect. The ascent up the mountain is very steep. A narrow door leads into the temple, which contains but one room. This apartment is barely large enough to allow the visitor to walk round the Siva stone. The temple presents an appearance of great strength, and, perched securely on its airy height, has long bid defiance to the all-destroying hand of Time. According to Abul Fazel's account, it was built by the vizier, Rajah Kubaret. This would carry back the date of the erection to a period of two thousand and eighty-six years. There is no resident in the temple; but a Brahmin, who lives in a village at the foot of the mountain, comes every morning with an offering of flowers. He never fails in this duty, and everything is kept perfectly neat.

Warm baths, which are rarely seen in India, are considered in Kashmir, in the cold season, a necessary comfort.

I have not yet spoken of the Kashmerian horses, which, however, deserve honourable mention, if not on account of their beauty, at least for their extreme sure-footedness. These horses are short and strong, and journey over the mountains with wonderful ease. Their motion, in ascending, is so gradual, that the rider is not conscious that they are making any extraordinary exertion, nor are they less skilful in descending. I have come down declivities, where, at every step, my horse trod on stones more than two feet high, without shaking me in the saddle.

Their mode of passing over smooth, wet, slippery descents, is still more admirable. Here, where an European would scarcely trust his own feet, he may securely confide in the instinct of his hardy mountain pony. When the trusty animal arrives at the top of the acclivity he draws his four feet together, and slides safely down. The moment he reaches the bottom, he springs steadily on his feet. I must confess that, at first, this mode of travelling seemed to place my safety on such slippery grounds, that I allowed a native to take precedence of me in the descents. But soon perceiving the ease with which the trip was made, I took the lead and found pleasure in this mode of travelling which reminded me of the skating and sleigh exercises of my boyhood.

The long-expected papers arrived at length from Lahore. They were written by the young Maha-rajah, Dalib Singh, and by his vizier, Hera Singh. The letters, couched in the sweetest words of friendship, were enclosed in a brocaded bag and sealed. They invited, or rather permitted me to set out for Lahore. I was told that every precaution had been taken for my safety on the way, and that my friends at Lahore could no longer renounce the pleasure of seeing me. My escort was to be increased; the necessary parwanahs had been dispatched, and everything prepared to do honour to the friend of the great sirdar. The Orientals never fail to lavish sweet words, and the writers of these letters seemed to wish to atone by their honied expressions, for the restriction that had been put on my departure. The season, as I have said, was far advanced. The snow on Soliman's mountain descended every day nearer to the plain, and I therefore determined to set about the preparations for my journey.

I sent a formal message to the Schaykh

Gulam Muhyiddin, informing him of my intention to depart. This was a mere ceremony, as he was well aware of the nature of the letters I had received. I appointed an early day for my farewell visit. My servants and suite were delighted at the prospect of returning to the warmer climate of their native soil, and on the morning that I visited the governor, they were all dressed in their gayest attire. Even my horse was made a sharer in the general festivity, and was caparisoned in gold-plated trappings, with a bunch of heron feathers on his head.

The ceremonial of the visit was the same as on former occasions. The governor poured himself forth in the warmest expressions of friendship, and declared that he was most anxious to gratify my every wish. With such assurances I took leave.

I received a letter next day from the governor, in which he lamented not being able to obey the dictates of his heart, and accompany me on my way. But the recent events at Lahore had given him so much to do, and besides it was the time of the safran feast, and his presence would be required in Kashmir. I accepted his apologies with very good grace. I could not persuade myself that the want of his presence would be a serious loss. Our parwanahs, or passports, were prepared, everything was in readiness, and casting a last look on "The happy valley," I turned my horse's head towards Lahore.

CHAPTER IX.

My journey towards Baba Talab—Island in the lake—Lake Ouller—Kashmir once a lake—Customs of the Hindoos on occasions of births, marriages, and deaths—The religion of the Sikhs—A modified Hindooism—The Sikh priests—The initiatory rites—Privileges enjoyed by the Hindoos of Ranodj—Difficulty of having a boar's head served at dinner.

My way lay through the passes of Bara Mulah and Uri, in the direction of the great lake, Baba Talab. The shores of the lake are wholly devoid of beauty. There is neither hamlet nor village to be seen around. The borders of the lake on one side are quite flat, whilst on the other, its waters wash the foot of a bleak, uncultivated mountain.

Not far from the shore is a little island, on which are the ruins of an ancient palace. It seems to have been a stately edifice, if we may judge from the great blocks of stone which are still visible in the depths of the lake.

We read in Ayen Ackbery that there lies near the borders of Little Thibet, a great lake, called Ouller. This lake is twenty-eight coss in circumference, and receives into its bosom the waters of the Behut, and the Jylum. This lake is evidently the Baba Talab. Ayen Ackbery adds further: "In the midst of this lake, the Sultan Zeinulabeddin built a magnificent palace, which was called Zeinlunk." It is the ruins of this palace that we now see. According to our computation of time, it must have been erected in the year 1405.

That Kashmir was once a lake, there can be no doubt, as there is abundant evidence that the water must have found an outlet through the Mulla pass. There are, besides, in the valley, many traces of volcanic eruptions. It would be unnecessary to repeat here what every European traveller has remarked, and what the natives of Kashmir daily relate.

On my way, I passed through many towns and villages, the names of which I omit, as I remarked nothing of importance in these places. The customs of a people are, perhaps, the most interesting subject to which the attention of the traveller can be directed. To be born, to marry, and to die, are looked upon as the three great events of a man's life. In the first and last case, he has no power of choice, and there are some who think he has very little in the second. Be this as it may, certain it is that births, marriages, and deaths, are looked upon in every country, civilized and uncivilized, as events of the utmost moment, and that, not alone to the persons immediately concerned, but to all friends and neighbours, and sometimes to those who are neither the one nor the other. When a child is born amongst the Hindoos of Upper India, the Brahmin who is in the habit of performing the religious ceremonies in the family is made acquainted with the event. He comes to the house, and brings with him a table, on which he writes with chalk the hour and minute of the child's nativity. For this he receives one rupee and four anas.

On the same day, the father expends ten rupees in the purchase of confectionary. All the friends and neighbours are invited; to each guest is given a handful of comfits, for which he presents the Brahmin with one or two pai. In six days after this ceremony the Brahmin returns, and brings a copy on paper of what he had written on the first day. For this nativity paper, he receives five, sometims, eleven rupees. The Brahmin generally gives the child a name on his first visit; but should the day be numbered amongst the "unlucky," he defers that part of the ceremony to a more propitious hour.

When a Hindoo father in Northern India is about to get his daughter married, there are certain ceremonial preparations made in his house. A pole, four yards in height, and five inches in diameter, is fixed upright in the middle of the floor; this is called the moru, and is generally made of mango-wood. It is painted with red earth, and upon the top is placed a straw dschapper, or roof, about three feet in circumference. At the foot of the moru is a karra, or cup, filled with water.

Those who are not fortunate enough to get a cup of the Ganges water, contrive at least to procure a few drops of the sacred stream to pour into their karra. Upon the lid of the cup, two betel nuts and thirty-two pais are laid. Around the karra a thread of red cotton is wound, and over the cup and dschapper is thrown a red cotton cloth. Two small wooden stands, not raised far above the floor, are intended for the support of lamps, by the light of which the Brahmins are to read portions of their sacred books.

All these preparations being completed, the bride and bridegroom are led forward. They sit at the foot of the moru, under the dschapper. Upon this, the Brahmin takes the corner of the shawl which the young man wears as a girdle, and ties it to the maiden's shawl. The priest now begins to read in the sacred books, upon which the bride and bridegroom rise, and walk seven times round the moru, after which they again resume their seats. The father of the bride now comes forward, takes the corner of his daughter's shawl, and lays it in the hand of the bridegroom, to whom he gives at the same time a betel nut, and some betel leaves, with water and money. He then turns to the father of the bridegroom, pours some water into his hands, and offers him the same gifts that he has already presented to his son. This present is accepted by the father of the bridegroom, who then gives it, with some of the Ganges water, as alms to the Brahmins. Not content with this, he gives them besides, according to his means, cows, money, pieces of stuff, &c., and promises at the same time to give a banquet to fifty Brahmins, to which he invites, besides all the members of his family, his friends and acquaintances.

It is a custom amongst the Khathery Hindoos to purchase, at the marriage of a daughter, a great quantity of confectionary. This is made into a pile, over which some money is scattered. Every member of the family receives a portion of these comfits; the rest is given to the barber. This barber is a very important personage, whose claims upon the gratitude of the household may be best understood by denominating him "a match-maker." Amongst the Khatherys of Lahore, the father of the bride distributes, on the day after her marriage, to each inhabitant of the town, some confectionary, the quantity being regulated by the wealth of the donor.

Of the burning of the dead I have already spoken; I shall now say something of the rites performed for the dying. When a member of a Hindoo family is about to depart this life, his relatives lay him on the earthen floor, which has been previously strewn with cow-dung and dulzi.* There is then placed in his mouth a small coin, some thei (sour milk), a piece of munka (red coral), with saed (honey), and a little Ganges water. Upon the breast of the dying person is laid flowers and a ring made of red and yellow cotton. These rites having been gone through, the sick man is considered fully prepared to meet his last hour. These ceremonies for the dying are practised alike by the followers of Vischnu and of Siva.

The religious ceremonies of the Sikhs are very different from those of the Hindoos. During my journey, I was encamped for a few

* Dulzi is the name of one of the wives of Krischna, as well as of the shrub, which is used in the ceremonies of the dying.

days near one of their temples, which afforded me an opportunity of observing their religious exercises. The Sikh priests read every day, aloud in the temple, a portion of their sacred books. Everybody is welcome to attend this lecture. The Sikh religion is a kind of Hindooism, but with some modifications. It does not restrict its followers to the eating of certain meats, though it forbids the use of beef, or tame swine. Tobacco-smoking is also discountenanced. The great point in which the Sikh differs from the Hindoo is in the rejection of the distinction made by caste. Amongst the Hindoos, the privileged Brahmins are alone allowed to read the sacred books; they only enjoy the privilege of addressing the Almighty directly, whilst amongst the Sikhs, the humblest man in society is taught to believe that his prayer is as acceptable before the throne of Mercy as that of his more wealthy brethren. Neither are the Sikhs image-worshippers. The founder of this religion must have perceived the political disadvantages arising from the distinctions induced by caste: still their religious code, founded upon pure deism, is full of absurdities. The appearance of the Sikh priest is exactly what one might expect in the minister of a war-like people. The tall blue turban, bound with an iron head-piece, the sabre, always close-girded to his side, his shield slung upon his back, and the long beard descending to his breast, give to this warrior-priest a highly picturesque aspect, recalling forcibly to the mind of Europeans the times of the crusaders.

The ceremony of initiation into the Sikh religion bears some resemblance to that of the Christian baptism. Water is poured on the head of the neophyte. In this water, the sign of a cross has been several times made with a knife. One of the natives, however, who had passed through this ceremony, assured me, that on his initiation, the water had been stirred in a circle, and that there was no rule prescribed on that point. After the ceremony of pouring the water has been performed, the priest takes some butter, atta, and djackery, which he boils together. This compound is called karau, and is given by the priest to his new disciple, who eats of it. If the neophyte be rich, there is sufficient karau prepared to allow of some being distributed amongst his friends and acquaintances. If poor, there is only enough for himself. It is scarcely necessary to add that the priest is paid for the karau.

The prescriptions of caste are often used by the Hindoos as a pretext for refusing services, which they are not inclined to perform. The Hindoos are, with some few exceptions, forbidden the use of flesh meat; to the Mahomedans pork alone is prescribed. That Radjputs and Djahts are allowed to eat the flesh they kill with their hunting weapons in the chase, is, of course, understood; but in case of necessity, they evade the law, by cutting off the head a sheep with a sabre. The Brahmins of Guscherat and Ranodj are allowed to eat fish. All Hindoos indiscriminately are permitted, when at the baths of Hardwar, to eat meat; but this indulgence is permitted only whilst they remain at this sacred spot. The Sikhs, who may be called reformed Hindoos, are not subjected to these restrictions, and are particularly fond of the flesh of the wild boar. Hindoos refuse even to touch the unclean meats, or the vessels in which they have been prepared, though during my many years residence in India, I have known very good Hindoos, when removed from observing eyes, lay aside these prejudices, and use the very utensils in which Christian food had been prepared. Europeans generally employ Mahomedan servants to wait at table, that the Hindoo prejudices may not be disturbed; but, as I have observed, these prejudices are often alleged as pretexts for annoying their masters.

When in Rutly, I shot a wild boar, the head of which I ordered, a few days afterwards, to be prepared for dinner. I was seated at table, when I heard a loud debate outside my tent, and in a few minutes my khidmatgar, a Mahomedan, who had accompanied me from Benares, came, and told me very angrily that he had been prevented bringing in the dish, because it contained a boar's head. This was exceedingly absurd, as he had repeatedly brought hams to table. Besides, if his religious code commanded him not to touch swine's flesh, the prohibition did not extend to the dish, which was of porcelain. The khidmatgar was aware of all this, and said that it was the munschi whom I had hired in the mountains, who had excited this uproar. He added, that if I commanded it, he would bring in the boar's head, in spite of all observations. This, of course, I would not require. One of the Hindoo servants would willingly bring in the head, but would not touch the dish, for now that a question involving caste had arisen, every one became suddenly scrupulous. If I had allowed the head to be brought in without a dish, the point would have been settled, but I did not wish to give the munschi this satisfaction. There was still a remedy. One of those Hindoos who are considered too low to be soiled by any pollution was called, and he brought in the dish. Peace was by this means restored, but the head, which had been, literally, a bone of contention, was so little agreeable to my palate, that I left it to my says, the groom, and his companions. These were Hindoos below caste.

As I was well aware that the disturbance caused about the boar's head did not arise from conscientious scruples, for we were then in the country of the Sikhs, but from a wish to annoy —I, on the following morning, assembled my servants, and pronounced judgment on my anti-swine-eating munschi, and his three fellow-rioters. I dismissed them from my service. Chuni Lahl seemed a good deal disconcerted by this summary proceeding. The dismissed munschi was a subject of Gulab Singh's, and might have become a useful colleague.

CHAPTER X.

Vezirabad—General Avitabelli—Extraordinary manner of discovering the true mother of a child—General Avitabelli's conduct during the revolt at Peshawur—I find an escort awaiting me at Koori—Rumours about General Ventura—Fresh accounts of Scheer Singh's death—Arrival at Lahore—Billeted in General Ventura's house—Visit to the Maha-rajah—Review—History of the Koh-i-noor.

General Avitabelli's position at the Sikh Court was rather a singular one. A Neapolitan by birth, he served, during a long time, in the French army. On peace being established in 1814, he went to India, and entered the service of Runjeet Singh. He is a stern soldier—one who can neither be intimidated nor moved. Here, in Vezirabad, he is feared and respected.

The following anecdote will give an idea of his shrewdness and his capability of governing the people amongst whom he resides:

A certain Mahomedan woman, of respectable family, resided in Peshawur at the time that General Avitabelli was governor of the place. This woman had a son and daughter. Both married, and the daughter and daughter-in-law gave birth, at the same time, to two children, one a boy, the other a girl. This circumstance gave a great deal of occupation to the mothers of the sick ladies. They were now become grandmothers, and many visits were exchanged in consequence of the important events that had occurred in their families.

Some time had passed over, the young mothers were again in perfect health, when a serious dispute arose between them. The daughter's child was a girl, that of the daughter-in-law a boy. The former maintained that the boy was hers, and had been taken from her, and given to her sister-in-law. The woman accused of having stolen the boy, denied the charge, and she was supported in her declara-

M 2

tion by her husband's mother. The strife became serious, and the contending parties brought the affair before the judge. This magistrate, who was no Solomon, not being able to elicit the truth, dismissed the complainants. The latter were not satisfied, and appealed to the high court, in which General Avitabelli presided.

The case was brought before him as he sat in the divan. Public curiosity was strained to the highest pitch, and each eagerly asked his neighbour: "How will the judge decide?" The statements upon both sides having been gone through, General Avitabelli ordered two goats to be brought, one having a male, the other a female kid. This being done, he sent for two sheep that had each a lamb, one a male, the other a female. In like manner, he commanded two cows to be brought, of which one had a male, the other a female calf. These different quadrupeds being introduced, he ordered that the goats, the sheep, and the çows should be milked, and the milk of each animal placed in a separate vessel, which should be marked. "Now," said the General, "let this milk be examined, and it will be found that that which belongs to the animals that have male young is stronger than the milk which has been taken from the others." Upon inspection, this was found to be correct. "Now," said the judge, "bring me some milk from the mothers of the children." The milk was brought, and General Avitabelli declared that the milk of the daughter was stronger than that of the daughter-in-law, and that, consequently, she must be the mother of the boy.

Whether General Avitabelli had any private information on the subject, which induced him to act as he did, or whether the difference in the milk was really so striking, I cannot say, but certain it is, that the wisdom of the judge astonished everybody, and his decision was universally admired.

I heard, from the general's own lips, a circumstance which proves the coolness and inflexibility of his character. During the time that he was Governor of Peshawur the troops revolted. The government-house, in which the general resided, was strong enough to resist for some time the attacks of troops, unprovided with cannon. The rebels made certain proposals, to which the general refused to give an answer, and threatened to shoot down, without mercy, any who dared to approach his dwelling. The troops, not wishing to enforce the fulfilment of this promise, retired to some distance, and pitched their camp. They intended to surround the place, and hoped that the general would be obliged to yield. But they reckoned without their host. General Avitabelli went into the gaols, and told the prisoners that, if they were willing to become soldiers, they should be declared free. The proposal was accepted, and robbers, murderers, thieves, and depredators of every kind, were presented with arms, and led out against the revolted troops. The latter were not a little surprised at seeing an army brought against them; and when it was proposed to them to lay down their arms, or submit to be shot, they preferred the former alternative, and returned to their duty.

When I arrived in Koori, I found there an escort of twenty sirwars sent from Lahore to conduct me on my way. I was to march next day as far as Schadirah, where Gulab Singh's regiments were stationed, and where it was reported that he was himself staying. This cunning fox was always afraid of having his abode discovered, and generally set afloat many contradictory reports, in order to deceive those whose presence he wished to shun.

His brother, Sutjid Singh, had been detected plotting against Hera Singh, in consequence of which he had been obliged to leave Lahore, and retire to Schadirah. Gulab went there to meet him and attempt a reconciliation between him and Hera Singh. In this he succeeded and Sutjid had returned to Lahore. It was at first said that he had gone into the English territories, and the appearance of some English troops on the banks of the Sutlej had alarmed the Sikhs. But all had been explained: these regiments had been removed from their quarters in consequence of fever having broken out there, and having carried off thousands.

Being now near the Sikh territory I constantly learned the current news of the day. Of General Ventura, it was said that he had not left the Sikh service, but had gone to Ferozepoor, to seek an interview with the English commander-in-chief, to explain some misunderstandings that had arisen.

The report of General Avitabelli having left the service was also contradicted. It was said that he was now at Delhi, and that Hera Singh had invited him to return to Lahore, promising him a higher post than that he had held under Scheer Singh. As he has not returned, it was to be supposed that he was not inclined to settle at Lahore. Many of my European acquaintances had left the Sikh capital. The young Frenchman, General Ventura's agent for the shawl trade, was dead.

I learned now every day fresh particulars concerning Scheer Singh's tragical death. The unhappy maha-rajah had been repeatedly warned against the Sandiwaliy, but to those who cautioned him, he always replied: "What more do you wish? He is my brother, he eats and drinks with me; would you wish us again to quarrel after having become friends?"

On my arrival at Schadirah, I was informed that Hera Singh had appointed me quarters at Anarkali. I was received on the left bank of the Ravi by the sirdar, Gurmuk Singh Lamba, who, after delivering the customary greetings in the name of the maha-rajah, and the vizier, proposed accompanying me to Anarkali. This was General Ventura's residence, but he was then absent, and nothing could be more disagreeable to me than the idea of being billeted in this manner. I suspected, moreover, that Hera Singh wished to profit by this opportunity to seize the general's house. I objected to going to Anarkali, and requested that I should be provided with some other residence. The officer pretended to comply with my desire, but returned after some time, saying that no other place could be found, and that Hera Singh *requested* me to accept the quarters he had provided.

There was now no alternative, and I was obliged to comply with this *request;* but what was my horror, on arriving at Anarkali, to find there Dr. and Mrs. Harvey, the guests of General Ventura, and at whose disposal he had left his house. I was glad to meet Dr. Harvey, whose acquaintance I had made during my former visit to Lahore. I felt, however, that he would be much happier at the other side of the Sutlej than here, where assassination and robbery were matters of daily occurrence. The presence of his wife and child must, in such circumstances, have been an additional cause of alarm. I was very much annoyed when I discovered all the inconvenience Dr. Harvey and his family had been made to suffer on my account. The officers who had been dispatched to prepare for my reception had wished to expel him altogether from the house. After many expostulations, he succeeded in dissuading them from this purpose; but then nothing would satisfy them but to seize the very rooms occupied by him and his family. It was in vain that he repeated his conviction that the other rooms of the house would satisfy me quite as well: these polite officers would not listen to any objection, and actually obliged him to quit his apartments.

Upon hearing this, I wrote to Hera Singh, and, after saluting him with the finest orientalisms, begged to announce my intention of abiding in my tent during Dr. Harvey's stay at Anarkali. I added that, looking upon the house as General Ventura's property, I could not think of forcing myself there as a guest during the absence of the master.

I was now returned to Lahore, after an absence of a few months, and how great were the changes that had taken place during that time. All seemed to feel as if the ground beneath their feet covered a volcano, an explosion of which might be every moment expected. Hera Singh shared in the general apprehension. He was solely dependant on the military, whose demands were daily becoming higher, as they felt their importance increasing. It was evident that Hera Singh's position was unsafe, and that all Gulab's shrewdness would be now needed to steer the bark which held the fortunes of the family safely through the dangerous passage, where a Charybdis yawned and a Scylla frowned.

Gulab was too crafty to appear upon the scene of action, but he directed all the movements of Hera Singh. If Gulab Singh's position and political skill secured to him great influence, this was in a great measure counterbalanced by prejudices founded on differences in religion. Gulab Singh's family are not Sikhs, and this circumstance was not forgotten by their enemies. The Sikhs proved in the war with Ahmed Schah, the influence that the spirit of bigotry has over them. Gulab Singh learned this, but spite of all his cunning, the discovery was made too late. He changed his religion, at least in appearance, and became a Sikh; but the star of his destiny had passed the culminating point, and his fortunes were irretrievable.

My interview with the little Maha-rajah Dalib Singh was gone through with the usual forms. Many beautifully-caparisoned elephants, driven by their respective mahouts, arrived early in the morning before my tent. With this escort I proceeded to the palace, where my coming was announced by the firing of cannon. The maha-rajah, with Hera Singh beside him, received me in the very spot where, a few months before, I had taken leave of Scheer Singh. The entire court was in mourning, and the beautiful white dresses produced a far more elegant effect than variegated robes could do. Rich thick silk and the most costly stuffs of Kashmir and Thibet were here displayed in all the graceful folds of the eastern costume, whilst the beauty of the material appeared to still greater advantage from the snowy whiteness of the hue. Dalib Singh, a little boy of between five and six years of age, played his part as well as could be expected. It was evident that the poor little child did not know who his master was. It was announced by Hera Singh, that, in compliment to me, the troops then in Lahore should be reviewed on the following day.

At the appointed hour, the elephants arrived; and, accompanied by Gurmuk Singh and another general, I set out. As we approached the palace, we met the little maha-rajah, accompanied by Hera Singh. We proceeded to the place selected for the review, where, when we arrived, the maha-rajah was greeted enthusiastically by the soldiers, all of whom, but especially the Sikhs, seemed devoted to him. Hera Singh paid me marked attention; and we parted on the most friendly terms, he taking his way to the palace, whilst I directed my course towards Anarkali.

What had passed between Hera Singh and me, concerning General Ventura's house, had not failed to excite remarks at court; and some of the most powerful nobles did not hesitate to say that measures ought to be taken against General Ventura. They said that he had received from Scheer Singh all his arrears of pay, and that he had now carried off in money, shawls and precious stones, amounting at least to six or seven lacs of rupees; besides, who could tell whether he would ever return, and whether he might not join the English? General Ventura was, indeed, looked upon in Lahore, as the most crafty of all the European generals, as it was universally thought that he had outwitted Hera Singh; but to the credit of the latter, I must say that he did not seem to entertain the slightest suspicion derogatory to the honour of General Ventura.

The proceedings of the Indian courts are so very different from those of Europe, that it is difficult for one unacquainted with the customs of the country to give an opinion on public matters. An anecdote which I heard at this time lately, illustrates very significantly the relations between the government and the army.

A certain Nabob of Murschedabad proposed a

question, and whoever should give a satisfactory answer was to receive a reward. The inquiry proposed was this: "What is it that did not happen last year, has not happened this year, and will not occur next year?" Learned men came from all parts of the kingdom to the nabob's court; for the prize to be awarded was a large one. Many an old gentleman rubbed his forehead and knitted his brows, and many a young man went farther, and slapped his head forcibly, as if he hoped by this concussion to excite greater activity in his brain. But all was in vain: the problem remained unsolved. At length a military officer stepped before the nabob, and greeting him with profound reverence, said: "O King! may you live a thousand years, as long as your father the sun, and as your mother the earth. You, O King, did not pay your troops last year, you have not paid them this year, nor do you intend to pay them next." This answer was deemed satisfactory, and the sepoy received the prize.

Nobody here ventures to discuss General Avitabelli's conduct. His name is always pronounced in an under tone. The awe that he inspired when Governor of Peshawur has not yet subsided. It was, at that time, feared that he would seize upon the province. When he returned to Lahore, and built the little fort in which he lives, fresh alarm was excited. It was then feared that he would invite over the English, and from the ramparts of his fort fire down on the natives. These reports, which were only whispered about, show what an impression he had made on the minds of the people.

The koh-i-noor again became a subject of general conversation. It was now reported that Gulab Singh had carried that, with many other treasures, to Jumbu. The history of the koh-i-noor would be sufficient to fill a volume. What commotion and what tears has it not caused! The events that led to its falling into the possession of Runjeet Singh are worth recording.

It is said that the koh-i-noor, and another diamond of equal size, were once used as eyes for a great idol at Mathura. The Moslems plundered the town. The koh-i-noor changed masters. It ceased to be the eye of an idol, and was transferred to the brow of some young and fair sultana. The chances of war soon placed "the mountain of light" in new hands. Battles had been fought, and cities had been depopulated for the sake of this gem. It at length became the property of the Moguls.

Nadir Schah came to Delhi, and did not forget to inquire for the koh-i-noor. The poor badschah wished to preserve the treasure, but a woman at length betrayed him. She told Nadir Schah that the badschah had secreted the jewel in the folds of his turban, which he did not lay aside day or night. This information having been further confirmed, Nadir Schah took his measures accordingly.

The day appointed for his departure from Delhi had arrived: a high festival was proclaimed, and every honour was paid to the guest, who when the day was closing rose to depart. The two kings poured themselves forth in expressions of the warmest friendship; nay more, they vowed to each other a brotherly love. In a burst of emotion Nadir Schah took from his head the tall Persian cap, in which the royal diadem was set, and round which numerous strings of costly pearls were twined, and proposed to the badschah an exchange of turbans. This amongst the Moslems is looked upon as the truest pledge of friendship; and the request, according to the customs of the country, could not be refused.

The dismay of the Great Mogul may be imagined; but these Eastern kings are so trained in the art of dissimulation, that the badschah made the exchange without apparent emotion. So great was his coolness, that Nadir Schah was uncertain whether he had attained the object of his wishes. He soon afterwards took leave, and on arriving in his tent commenced to unfold the turban. His doubts now ceased, for within the innermost fold he found the koh-i-noor. This wonderful treasure remained long in the possession of the Persian, but was afterwards transferred to the Cabul dynasty.

After a long chapter of accidents, the koh-i-noor was brought to Lahore in 1812, by Schah Schujah, when he sought the protection of Runjeet Singh. Runjeet had heard a great deal of the stone, and though he was no judge of jewels, he earnestly desired the possession of this one, and was determined to leave no means untried to gratify his wishes.

Wuffa Begum, the wife of Schah Schujah, lived at Schadirah. Runjeet sent to demand the jewel of her, but she declared that she had it not.

This answer did not satisfy the Sikh; he ordered that all her jewels should be seized, and brought to Lahore. Many of these were of such great beauty, that Runjeet believed that the koh-i-noor must be amongst them; but having afterwards discovered his error, he ordered the begum to be closely watched. Nobody was allowed to go in or out of her palace without being searched; and Runjeet let her know that nothing would satisfy him but the possession of the koh-i-noor.

The begum sent him a beautiful ruby. This stone exceeded in splendour anything the maha-rajah had ever seen, and he now believed that he really beheld the koh-i-noor. But as he was himself unable to estimate the value of jewels, he sent for a man who was conversant in such things, and who besides had seen the great "mountain of light." The Sikh displayed befere the connoisseur a great number of jewels, and asked which of these was the koh-i-noor? The man replied that the koh-i-noor was not amongst these stones, and that all he saw there were insignificant, compared with that great gem.

Runjeet's anxiety to possess this treasure was now greater than ever. He tried what starvation could do, but the begum endured the trial unmoved. He then changed his mode, and tried persuasion and arguments. The begum promised to give the koh-i-noor, if her husband, who was then imprisoned at Lahore, should be set free. This was done, but some other conditions of the agreement were left unfulfilled. Runjeet demanded the jewel; the begum said that it had been pledged to a merchant in Kandahar. This was an evasion. Starvation was again tried, but in vain. New severities were about to be exercised, when the Schah promised that on a certain day, the koh-i-noor should be delivered to Runjeet Singh.

The day appointed for this important transfer was the 1st of June, 1813. The maha-rajah came to the place of meeting, accompanied by some trusty friends, nor did he forget to bring connoisseurs, to whose inspection the jewel should be submitted. When the Sikhs entered the hall where the schah and his friends were assembled, mutual greetings were exchanged, after which a death-like stillness prevailed. An hour passed in this manner, when Runjeet, who was impatient, made a sign to one of his friends, intimating a desire that he should remind the schah of the object of his visit. The schah made a signal to a slave, who retired, and returned in a few minutes with a little packet which he laid on the carpet, at an equal distance from the maha-rajah and the schah. Having done this, he returned to his place, and all were again silent. There is no saying how long the company might have remained mute, if Runjeet had not made a sign to one of his adherents, who, rising, lifted the packet, unfolded the wrappings, and revealed the koh-i-noor. The precious gem was recognised by those who had come for that purpose, and the maha-rajah was satisfied. Delighted at the sight of this splendid prize, he turned to the schah, and inquired what the stone was worth. The answer was, "Djuty."

This word djuty has many significations. It means shoes, and is used in India to express the infliction of a disgraceful and deserved punishment. "I will give thee shoes," "I will beat thee with shoes," is a threat that implies the utmost contempt. Besides this, djuty, or dhjuty, has other meanings, which may be expressed by a slight difference in the pronunciation. In one sense, it implies lies, deceit, disgrace, treachery, insult, mockery, jesting. In another sense the word signifies war, battles, &c. The koh-i-noor has since changed masters;* let us hope that its future history will be more peaceful than the past has been.

An eye-witness of the meeting between the

* When the young Rajah Dalib Singh was recognized by the English government, a resident and some English troops were stationed at Lahore. The Sikh troops revolted, the koh-i-noor fell into the hands of the English as their share of the booty, and was sent to London. It formed, as every one is aware, one of the features of the Great Exhibition of 1851.

schah and the maha-rajah, told me that the dignified and composed deportment of the former made a profound impression on all present. Even Runjeet Singh, whose feelings were not very refined, did honour to the strength of mind manifested by the fallen prince.

CHAPTER XI.

Position of affairs at Lahore—Power of the soldiery—Threatened danger to myself—Preparations to leave Lahore—Hera Singh's advice—Farewell visit to the Maha-rajah—Some account of his ancestors—Runjeet Singh's love for horses—Departure from Lahore—Arrival at Ferozepoor—I leave for Ludiana—My cooking utensils mislaid—I become ill—Kindness of the English physicians—I change my route and determine to visit Delhi and Hardwar.

THE state of public affairs at Lahore was really alarming. The government, which had once ruled the solidiers, now stood in awe of them. Hera Singh and all the great nobles trembled at the slightest symptom of dissatisfaction in the many-headed hydra which they were trying to guide, but were unable to govern.

I fancy that Gulab Singh and his nephew would have willingly closed the portals of misrule, which they had thrown open when they enticed the soldiers from their duty. Nothing would now satisfy the army; the gratification of one request was only a ground for new demands. The riches of Dehan Singh and his family must have been immense if Hera could have held his position under such circumstances.

One day, when I was leaving the palace, where I had had an audience, and just at the moment that I was about to mount my elephant, a servant whispered something in the ear of Chuni Lahl. In a few minutes, Gurmuk Singh Lamba, who had conducted me from the durbar, came up. From intelligence he had received, it was deemed prudent to change my route. I was accordingly conducted to my abode by a circuitous way, and then informed that my escort had apprehended an attack.

I was anxious to leave Lahore, and Hera Singh advised me to take the shortest road that led to the English possessions. This was through Ferozepoor. Relays of cavalry were to be provided along the way, that my journey might be performed with greater expedition.

Nothing now detained me at Lahore. I had made my farewell visit to the maha-rajah, and had taken a friendly leave of Hera Singh. This may not be an unfavourable opportunity to say a few words of the ancestors of the baby-ruler, who now sits on the throne of Lahore.

The Sikh sect was founded by Guru Manak. Guru Govinda is the first Sikh warrior that we find opposing the Mahommedans in the Punjab; and long and bloody were the contests between them. During the latter half of the eighteenth century, Churut Singh, son of Noudh Singh, distinguished himself as a Sikh leader. He obtained, in 1761, permission to build a mud fort in Gujarawala. This was of great advantage to him, as it served as a place of refuge for his family and adherents, as well as a stronghold in which they could secure their plunder. The whole life of Churut Singh was continued warfare against the government at Lahore, and against Ahmed Schah. In these contests, he experienced the various chances of war, sometimes conquering, and being sometimes defeated. In 1764, a son was born to him, who received the name of Maha Singh.

The Sikhs had now become a great power, and were divided into twelve missulhy, or clans, able to bring an army of seventy thousand horse into the field. These clans chose one amongst their chiefs, distinguished for his understanding and valour, who was to guide the other sirdars, all of whom, however, were still considered his equals. Each chief received a title, which was either the name of a place under his jurisdiction, or a name significant of some important event in his life.

These missulhy were :

	Horsemen.
1. Bhangy Missul, under Harry Singh, Schande Singh, and Gunda Singh, furnishing .	10,000
2. Ramgurrüch, Missul under Jessa Singh Thoka . .	3,000
3. Ghuneyah Missul, under Jy Sing	8,000
4. Nuckeyah Missul, also under Jy Singh	2,000
	23,000

	Horsemen.
Brought forward . .	23,000
5. Alluwallah Missul, under Jessah Singh Rullat . .	3,500
6. Dullawallicah Missul, under Tarra Singh Ghybah . .	7,500
7. Nischanwalliah Missul, under Sangul Singh and Mohur Singh	12,000
8. Fyulapuriah Missul, under Kuppur Singh and Kusiah Singh	2,500
9. Krora Singhiah Missul, under Krora Singh and Bhugais Singh	12,000
10. Schahid and Nehung Missul, under Kurmuk Singh and Gurbukh Singh	2,000
11. Phulkiah and Bhykiah Missul under Rajah Otta Singh	5,000
12. Luxur - Chukiah Missul, under Churut Singh . .	2,500
Total . .	70,000

Churut Singh, who had distinguished himself in various battles, died in 1774, in consequence of the bursting of his matchlock. He was at the time engaged in a war with the Rajah of Jumbu, or Jumnu, whose son, Bridj Radjdeo, had rebelled against him, and with whom Churut Singh had formed an alliance.

Churut was succeeded by his son, Maha Singh. The boy was only ten years old, and during his minority the kingdom was governed by his mother and Jy Singh. When he attained the age of seventeen, he took the reins of government into his own hands. He ruled with foresight and prudence, and acquired great influence in the Punjab. In 1780, a son was born to him, who received the name of Runjeet Singh. Maha Singh died in 1792, and Runjeet succeeded his father in the possession of Missul Gujarawalla, under the guidance of his mother. In 1795, he married the daughter of Gurbuk Singh and Suddakour, granddaughter of Jy Singh. In 1798, he assumed sovereign power, ably supported by the enterprizing spirit, and extraordinary talents of his mother-in-law, Suddakour. To her aid he was indebted for much of his success, and one of the blackest stains upon his character is the ingratitude with which he treated this woman. Guided by her counsels, he conquered Lahore in 1799; and in a short time afterwards, we find Suddakour flung into prison by his orders. The monotony of a captive's life was intolerable to her active spirit; she tore her hair, beat herself violently on the head and breast, and called a thousand times on death to terminate that prison solitude, which to her "quick bosom," was "a hell."

But a crime of a darker nature, though perhaps accompanied with less cruelty in the execution, stains the memory of Runjeet Singh. Heedless of the ties of natural affection, and insensible to every feeling of humanity, like another Nero, he ordered his own mother to be murdered. And yet one of the eulogiums that I have heard pronounced upon him, was that he never shed blood wantonly. It would be difficult to reconcile the assassination of a mother with such laudation. Besides, many executions took place in his reign, which if he did not order, he sanctioned. Runjeet's son, Karrak, was born in 1801. In the following year, the Sikh chief took Amrit Sir, and founding in one place a fort, in another a city, gradually became master of the kingdom of the Punjab. We now find him seated as maha-rajah on the throne of Lahore, governing arbitrarily but steadily. He was the founder of the Sikh empire, and it is universally admitted that he was beloved by his subjects.

Amongst his peculiarities, may be reckoned his love for horses. It is well known that a dispute about a horse was the cause of a war with Cabul and Peshawur. He had the handsomest horses for his own use, and eschewed elephants and palanquins, until the infirmities of illness obliged him to use them. Everybody has heard of the clumsy, shabby coach sent to him as a present by the English rulers in India. The coachman's seat was placed high, in front of this awkward vehicle. The only remark that Runjeet Singh was ever known to make on the subject of this valuable gift was: "What strange people these Europeans must be; they give the driver an agreeable, advantageous position, and place themselves low behind him."

The Rani (queen) Mashoul Kour was delivered of twins in 1806. This rani was Suddakour's second daughter. It was said that in the case of these twins she imposed upon her husband; that her own child was really a daughter, and that she purchased these two boys, of whom one was said to be the son of a weaver, the other of a carpenter. However this might be, their claims were never questioned by Runjeet, and the one was called Scheer, the other, Tara Singh.

In 1821, a son was born to Karak Singh. This child received the name of Nonehal Singh.

Runjeet Singh had many illegitimate children: amongst others, Peschuwara and Kaschmira Singh; but in 1839, Dalib Singh, the son of his wife, was born. Runjeet was succeeded by his son Karak, a prince of too mild a character to be admired by the Sikhs. I have never heard him praised, and yet, everything that I have learned of his conduct was calculated to give me a good opinion of him. He reigned but one year, and died, it is said, of poison. His son, Nonehal, succeeded. This prince was of a more warlike disposition than his predecessor. It is a custom in India, that a son, after assisting at his father's funeral rites, should bathe in the river. Nonehal Singh having been present at the burning of his father's body, went to take the prescribed bath. Having performed this duty, he returned to the city; . but just as he was passing under the great gate-way, a beam fell from the arch, and killed him on the spot. Though Gulab Singh was the avowed enemy of the maha-rajah it happened that his son Urjum was, at that moment, in his company, and shared his fate. Karak Singh's widow was about to become a mother, and the succession could not be settled until the birth of her child. In the meantime, Scheer Singh was appointed regent, and remained in undisturbed authority, for the unhappy rani was one morning found strangled, her child having never seen the light. Scheer Singh was accused of being the contriver of this assassination, whether justly or unjustly, it would be difficult to say. His own death, the circumstances of which have been already narrated, was not less awful. He was succeeded by Dalib Singh, Runjeet's youngest son. This child's birth was so unexpected that doubts of his legitimacy were entertained by many; but several of the natives with whom I have spoken on the subject, declare him to be miniature likeness of the great Runjeet.

The Sikh forces, under Runjeet Singh, amounted to more than eighty-two thousand men, and three hundred and seventy-six pieces of cannon. These troops are not all regular, and the number acquainted with European tactics is very small indeed. The whole Sikh army was completely annihilated by the English at the battle of Sobraon.

Scheer Singh was suspected of being accessory to the death of Karak and Nonehal Singh. His being their successor forms the sole grounds for this suspicion; but I must confess that I should not be inclined to accept this opinion without clearer evidence. Scheer Singh, though reared in an Eastern court, was too thoughtless to be a plotter; and it is probable that the contriver of these changes remained far from the scene of action. The conspiracy to which Scheer Singh fell a victim had been long arranged. When, eight months before the fatal catastrophe, he visited the mountains, a report of his death was circulated, and a short time afterwards it was rumoured that he was very ill, and even laid upon the earth—a ceremony observed by the Sikhs as well as the Hindoos. These reports were forerunners of the catastrophe, and intended probably to ascertain the state of public feeling.

Scheer Singh had been advised by General Ventura to master that Radjput family which had risen into too great power. This counsel was deemed good for many reasons; but Scheer Singh deferred putting it into execution until the Dasserah festival, when he expected that Gulab Singh would come to Lahore. As that wily chief seldom ventured out of his mountain fastnesses, it would be difficult to catch him; but it was supposed that the approaching festival would induce him to visit the Sikh capital. The death of Pertab Singh was contrary to the wishes and plans of Dehan Singh, who wished to proceed step by step, and so gradually to attain his object. Neither he nor any of his family could sit on the throne, not being Sikhs.

Amid friendly wishes and affectionate farewells I left Lahore. Those of my suite who had accompanied me from Hindoostan, seemed delighted at leaving the Punjab. They anticipated with no slight degree of satisfaction the importance they should enjoy in their own country in relating their adventures in "the land of wonders." This is the reputation that Kashmir enjoys in India.

In Ferozepoor, which is only a few days' march from Lahore, I had the pleasure of meeting my friend Bernard, who was stationed there with his regiment. General Ventura was there too, with a great deal of baggage.

Having passed some days at Ferozepoor, I set out for Ludiana. I did not intend to remain there, and sent my tent on two days' journey in advance. As I had ordered relays of horses, I knew that I should easily overtake the bearers. Upon arriving at the place where my tent was pitched, it was discovered that my *batterie de cuisine* had, through some oversight, been sent on with the rest of the luggage. Such mistakes are of frequent occurrence in India; but as a traveller ought not to be squeamish, it is better that he should accustom himself betimes to the same food as the natives are satisfied with. I sent to the neighbouring bazaar to purchase cooking utensils; the meal was prepared, but in about ten minutes after I had partaken of it I was seized with violent pains in every part of my body. I became seriously unwell, but though not much better on the following day, I set out on my journey.

In four days I reached Ludiana. I was now completely exhausted. I lay in my bed, without even sufficient energy to order medical attendance to be sought for. It so happened that one of my servants accidentally met one of the English physicians residing in the town. This gentleman immediately visited me, and to him I owe a debt of gratitude that I shall never forget. But for his aid, and that of one of his professional friends, to whom he introduced me, it is probable that I should never have left Ludiana. During many weeks, I continued very ill, and when the severity of the attack had abated, I found my strength completely prostrated. This extreme weakness obliged me to alter the route I had purposed to take. My intention had been to travel down the Indus to Bombay, and there to embark for Europe. I had written to the Governor-General, Lord Ellenborough, to acquaint him with my plan, and had received the most friendly assurances that everything should be done to facilitate my progress.

My illness had been of such long duration, that the warm weather had commenced before I could make preparations for my departure. Under these circumstances, it would be unwise to travel southwards; I, therefore, resolved to return to the mountains, and pass the warm months there. Before entering the hilly country, I determined to visit Delhi once more; and as this was the year in which the great mela, or fair, was to be held at Hardwar, I deemed that place, too, worthy of a visit.

CHAPTER XII.

I visit Delhi again—Sad recollections—Shah Jehan and Aurungzib—Hardwar—Sanctity of the place—The mela, or fair—Enormous elephant—Hindoo women—Religious rites—Krischan-boys—Offerings in money—The Brahmins—Donations to the Ganges—The Fakirs — Their extravagant conduct — Pomp of the temples during the mela—I leave Hardwar and proceed to the mountains.

IT was evening when I reached Delhi. I had passed the day under some beautiful plantain trees, my munschi having gone on before to hire a dwelling in the city. The entrance to Delhi from this side is handsomer than the approach from Agra, an advantage it owes to the beautiful and majestic trees with which the environs are planted.

I passed some weeks at Delhi; but this time I was not employed either in antiquarian researches, or in historic reminiscences. The traveller coming from foreign lands to view the great monuments of antiquity, often finds his curiosity extinguished by feelings arising from his personal experience. The desolation that reigned in Delhi accorded but too well with the state of my own mind; and the inscription on the palace walls—

"IF THERE BE AN ELYSIUM ON EARTH,
IT IS THIS, IT IS THIS,"

seemed the saddest mockery, where the descendant of the great Tamerlane sits on the throne of his ancestors, a dependant on the British government. The lessons of the moralist on the instability of human things, deduced from the wreck of nations, never comes so forcibly home to the heart as when, under the pressure of sorrow, we view the remains of bye-gone glory. When the golden cup, in which the sweet affections of the heart sparkled like purest wine, has been dashed to the earth, we feel companionship with desolation, and partnership with decay. It is then we understand the dejection of that spirit which, bowed to the dust, said to the worm, "thou art my brother," and to corruption, "thou art my sister."

So much has been said of the past and present history of Delhi, that it seems almost superfluous to add a word. The modern city was built by Schah Jehan, father of the mighty Aurungzib, who may be looked upon as the last "Great Mogul." Everything about the present emperor seems a mockery: a puppet in the hands of a foreign power, he has been but too truly called "the shadow of a king." The celebrated peacock throne, covered with jewels, which was carried off by Nadir Schah in 1739, has been replaced by one gilt and enamelled, ornamented with figures of the peacock.

I left Delhi, and proceeded towards Hardwar, where I intended to remain until the termination of the great mela, after which I purposed to ascend the mountain regions, and remain there for some months.

The reputed sanctity of Hardwar arises from

the Saga, which relates that Krischna bathed in the Ganges at this spot. It is here that this mighty stream, leaving the mountain tracts, enters into Hindostan Proper. The water is not very deep in this part at the season when the fair is held; and as alligators do not come up so far, the place offers many conveniences to the pilgrims, who every year flock thither from all parts of India. The great mela, or fair, is held every twelfth year, being the period of Jupiter's revolution round the sun. When Jupiter is in Aquarius and the sun in Aries, the mela commences. When on a former occasion I visited Hardwar, I heard a description of the scenes presented during the festival, but nothing that the imagination could picture could come up to the reality. The number of persons present at the time of my visit was computed at eighty thousand, but this, I am sure, fell far short of the truth.

Besides the pious Hindoos, who come here to perform their ablutions and make their offerings, the spirit of gain attracts dealers from every part of India. What a varied scene is then presented to the beholder! What a fanciful contrast in the style and colours of the costumes! What a striking difference in the cast of features, and expression of the various countenances! At the ghât the pious pilgrim who has travelled hundreds of miles to plunge into the sacred stream, is wholly employed in the performance of his religious rites. If we travel a little farther up the street, we find the crafty chapman, disputing the price of a horse or elephant. And I must here do justice to the animals I saw exposed for sale at Hardwar.

The horses of Affghanistan and the Bukhara ponies attracted my especial attention, nor were the prices asked extravagant. I was very sorry that I could not ascertain the exact height of an elephant which I saw at this fair, and which was the largest animal of the species I had ever seen.

The price of elephants varies very much. An animal newly-caught may, in some districts, be purchased for two hundred and fifty rupees. In the neighbourhood of Delhi, an elephant is estimated at eight hundred rupees, in the Punjab at twelve hundred; but the elephant I saw at Hardwar was valued at twenty thousand. I thought the sum enormous, but it was whispered, in confidence, that a handsome young female slave was to accompany the elephant. This, I believe, to be a falsehood, for slaves, male or female, are seldom sold in India. The merchant probably intended the story as a hoax.

At the earliest dawn, Hindoo women of the higher classes come to perform their ablutions. Many a lovely maiden may be seen at this hour, some conducted by their mothers, others in groups, attended by their servants. Pride and timidity induce them to come thus early, that they may avoid the prying eye of curiosity. The sun once fairly above the horizon, every half-hour brings increased pressure, hurry, and confusion; and the noise becomes momentarily greater by the bellowing of oxen, the sound of musical instruments, the voice of the mahout calling to his elephant, and, rising sharply above all, the wild cry of the fakir is occasionally heard. Thousands of bathers are continually pressing towards the ghats, where so many enter the river at the same time, and are so closely wedged together, that the water is sometimes completely hidden from a spectator on the bank.

At different distances up the river, platforms, three or four feet square, are erected. These rise about two inches above the level of the water, and are occupied by a number of little boys, dressed in robes of red muslin, and wearing caps *à la* Krischna. These children are looked upon as representatives of the god, and are appointed by the priests to receive the offerings of the faithful. The sums of money laid on these platforms are enormous. As each bather finishes his ablutions, he approaches the platform, lays down his offering, and the little Krischna gives him in return a piece of paint, with which he marks upon his forehead the horizontal or perpendicular lines that denote his caste.

As money is not disregarded in these religious services, the rich Hindoo performs his devotions with much greater pomp than his poorer neighbour. The man of wealth fixes his tent apart, and when he goes to bathe is accompanied by two Brahmins, one on either side, who conduct him with solemnity into the river, when, having plunged him three times beneath the sacred wave, they lead him back with the same state. The humbler votaries look with reverence on the man who is thus honoured by the society of beings whom they almost adore.

But these rites are not with all solely a religious ceremony. Many enjoy the bath for itself alone. These having fulfilled the prescribed forms, having flung themselves three times with outstretched hands prostrate on their faces in the stream, and performed the other duties, move about in the water, and enter into conversation with their neighbours. Whole groups may be seen walking about in this manner, chatting and amusing themselves. I must not forget to add that every bather, besides the offering made to the little Krischnas, drops something into the stream. This donation is according to the wealth of the individual. Some throw in a gem, others a piece of gold—some an ana, or a few pais.

The conduct of the fakirs during the mela cannot fail to amuse the stranger, though the awe-struck Hindoo multitude regard it with profound reverence. These hypocrites or enthusiasts, whichever they may be, seek above all things to attract public attention. They always bathe in the middle of the day, when the throng is greatest, and various are the decoys which their vanity prompts them to employ to catch the public eye. Some of them proceed to the ghats quite naked, which is the more shocking, as the Hindoos are very careful not to offend against modesty. Others go to the bath with a single piece of cloth wrapped round their bodies, and their hair dressed *à la* Fata, in imitation of Shiva. Some of these pious beggars streak their bodies with white paint, whilst others distinguish themselves by walking into the Ganges in full dress.

Let it not be supposed that the fakirs take their bath simply and singly like the rest of the community. By no means. Many of the chiefs of the fakirs abide constantly at Hardwar; and on the occasion of the mela, their disciples from all parts of India collect round them. All these religious corporations proceed together to the ghats, and, long before they become visible to those near the river, their approach is announced by yells such as one might expect to hear from the beasts of the forest. As they approach, the crowd fall back, and a passage is opened for them to the bathing-place. What a scene does that procession present! Groups of men, in fantastic costumes, some partly, others entirely naked, flourishing heavy clubs above their heads, and uttering wild cries, dance round their chiefs; and so they hurry on, until they reach the most public ghat. Here they rush tumultuously into the river, and hair is cleansed on the occasions of the great mela, and bodies purified, which has not been brought into contact with water for many years before. Many of the self-sufficient fakirs do not consider any water but that of the Ganges worthy to touch their sacred persons, so that thousands of these pious men, who live in remote parts of India, seldom enjoy the luxury of the bath. This privation must be the more sorely felt, as their hair is sometimes allowed to grow until it touches the feet. All these things considered, it must be supposed that those who bathe earliest find the water purest.

During the festival, the temples are decked with the greatest pomp. Lamps are constantly burning, bells ringing unceasingly, and the idols from morning until evening are surrounded by votaries. In the streets most remote from the ghats, the sound of cymbals is heard, and troops of dancing-girls are to be seen in their many-coloured costumes. Making an allowance for the difference in complexion, language, and dress, this mela bears a close resemblance to one of our German fairs.

An English magistrate, having under his command a considerable police force, remains at Hardwar during the time of the mela; and a military detachment is encamped on a little island in the river. This is not agreeable to the bathers, but it is considered a necessary precaution for the maintenance of order.

The mela having come to a close, I quitted Hardwar, and continued my route to the mountains. Here I passed the warm months, and then proceeded on my way towards Bengal.

CHAPTER XIII.

Burhampoor—Colonel Cathcart—Ruins of the ancient palace—Neatness of the houses—Beautiful Ghats—Gold and silver lace—Ahedlabab—Phootla, or Pootla—Dellegaon—Fardepoor—Adjinta—The rock temples—Antiquity of these excavations—By whom constructed—The great reservoir—Similarity of these structures with those of Egypt—Time employed in their erection—Number of workmen — Calculation of expense — Different ages of these Lehnas, or Temples—Distinct styles of architecture—Grim idols—Flat and arched-roof temples.

Still travelling southward, I arrived at Burhampoor, and visited with Colonel Cathcart the garden and fort and the ancient palace, once so extensive and so magnificent, now a heap of ruins. Colonel Cathcart was a most agreeable companion. His unchanging cheerfulness and the vivacity of his conversation were so very un-English, that I could not help thinking him very much superior to any of his countrymen I had ever met. In the course of our acquaintance, I made some observation to this effect, when he told me that his mother was French, and his father Scotch.

From the palace there is a fine view of the river, east and west; and directly opposite lie many beautiful gardens and mausoleums. The best preserved building is a haman, or warm bath. It is one of the largest I have seen in India, and needs but some slight repairs to be in as good a condition as ever.

The chief personages of the place paid me visits of ceremony, which politeness required that I should return. This gave me an opportunity of seeing the interior of the houses, the neatness and elegance of which surprised me. Having seen the antiquities of the place, I visited the different beautiful ghats that lie along the river, and which are well worthy of the traveller's attention. There is gold and silver lace manufactured in Burhampoor, which is used as trimming for turbans, &c. Several of the looms in which this lace is made, are established in a garden near the town, and the deep leafy shade afforded by the trees, renders the position very agreeable to the workmen.

A handsome mosque, wrought in massive hewn stone, is appointed as a residence for the European officers. It is a fine building, surrounded with a handsome court. A march of four coss brought me from Burhampoor, or Burrampoor as it is here called, to the village of Andoli. Six coss farther on lies Ahedlabab. The surrounding country is little cultivated. At about half an hour's journey there is a tolerably large river. Behind the village, on a slight elevation, there is a fort, of which the out-works are falling to decay. The bazaar is insignificant; and when I inquired for workmen to repair some of my travelling furniture that had been injured, I was informed that they had all gone to an adjoining town.

Phootla, or Pootla, a tolerably large village, lies about seven coss from Ahedlabab. It belongs to the Company, and is under the jurisdiction of the Bombay Presidency. The little villages through which I passed offered no attraction; and all presented pretty much the same aspect. From Phootla, I travelled seven coss to Dellegaon. The bazaar here was a little larger than in the other villages. All were surrounded by a mud wall, more or less high.

As I was travelling along the road, I met two gentlemen coming from Bombay. They were on horseback, and were proceeding to Agra to join the 64th regiment, to which they belonged. They had very little luggage, and I could not help admiring the simplicity of their appointments. How different from the proceedings of the same class of people in Hindoostan, where every one seems incapable of helping himself.

Leaving Dellegaon, I passed on to Fardepoor, a village about a coss and a half further off. Between Fardepoor and Adjinta, about one coss to the west of the latter place, within the enclosure of a deep valley, there is an amphitheatre of rock; and this, the ancient Buddhist inhabitants of the country fashioned into a number of temples. The works which I saw here excited my admiration and astonishment in the highest degree, and reminded me vividly of impressions that I had seen on copper coins in different parts of India, through the Burman empire, and in Java.

These rock buildings do not appear at first sight to be of such great antiquity as we are generally inclined to believe, and this opinion is heightened by the appearance of the paintings with which some of them are adorned. I know no solid grounds, however, on which I could support it; and all I mean to say is, that the first impression produced by the sight of these temples does not awaken an idea of their belonging to those very remote ages, with which common belief is apt to identify them. But the freshness of the paintings is no argument against their antiquity, as these may be ornaments belonging to a later period. The situation of the place, near and around which there are no cultivated tracts of land, nor any trace that such ever have been, the absence of water being an irremediable obstacle, implies that the contrivers of these temples sought only solitude. Besides this, the road from the valley to the temples is executed with so little care as to leave no doubt that it could never have been intended as a means of frequent communication. It appears to me much more probable, that these temples were fashioned at a period when the followers of Buddhism were persecuted by some other sect. In this retirement they might have found repose, and freedom for the fulfilment of their religious rites.

I have passed whole days in these lehnas, or rock-temples, my tent, or rather my carpet, spread out directly in front of the great reservoir, above which, at a distance of several hundred feet, a vast ridge of rock projected. Here I passed my time drawing. Above the overhanging rock, there are a few small houses, which, collectively, bear the name of Lehnapoor. These houses cannot be seen from the valley, neither are they visible from the temples.

The great reservoir seems to have been formed by the hand of nature; it is, I have been assured, of unfathomable depth. This reservoir, or pond, is so sheltered that one might be in the vicinity without perceiving it, either from the rock above or opposite. This was the case with myself, but my people, who were less attracted by the beauty of the lehnas than I, made the discovery of the tank.

This pond, or reservoir, which is about forty-five feet in diameter, is filled with the coolest water, in which are found fish weighing four or five pounds each. Upon the great rock which overhangs the tank, innumerable swarms of bees have plied their busy toil; and it is no exaggeration to say that crevices in the rock are filled with wax to the depth of several feet, and great masses are seen hanging from the ledge.

But to return to the temples. Those in the centre of the sweep can be reached by a nearer path, which, however, requires a skilful climber. This way leads to temple No. 4, but a more frequented though longer path leads to Nos. 15 and 16. As I before remarked, everything here proves that the persons who designed these buildings sought solitude and seclusion. Upon a closer examination, the similarity between these edifices and those of Egypt is very striking. What a host of conjectures does not the likeness awaken! The blending of styles of architecture belonging to two different regions of the earth, could not be accidental, and the inquisitive traveller feels himself irresistibly impelled to inquire the "how and when this was done;" but in these temples no traces remain that can solve the question. Nor has all that has yet been written about Egypt served to cast a clearer light on the history of her pyramids and her tombs. One conclusion may be, I think, safely drawn: the giant buildings of Egypt were the creations of tyrants, or of private individuals, whilst the rock-temples of India are evidently the result of the combined efforts and the unanimous wishes of a people. If we admit that the followers of Buddha were the founders of these temples, as well as of those in Ceylon, and the many similar erections throughout India, may we not be allowed to look upon these Buddhists as a great confraternity of skilful architects, painters, and sculptors? This may be carrying a supposition too far, but it is evident that they wished to surround their devotional rites with every charm that the arts placed at their disposal.

In looking at these temples, one is inclined to

believe that their formation required the united efforts of a nation, or that if the number of hands employed was small, the length of time that elapsed before their completion must have extended to centuries. But this opinion I hold to be groundless, and this will appear more evident if we consider that the number of workmen who could labour simultaneously at one of these temples must depend on the size of the excavation, which being in the commencement small, would not allow scope for the operations of many. No comparison could be made between the numbers needed in such an undertaking, and those that would be required for the erection of an ordinary building, or rather of an edifice, however large, built after the ordinary mode, where from the foundation to the roof, stone is laid upon stone. In the erection of the rock-temples, the operations of the workmen were also circumscribed by the fact of there being but one entrance, and this made the labours of one in a great measure dependent upon the progress of the other. One could on this account more easily estimate the number of persons employed in hewing out one of these temples. I do not mean the number that actually were employed, but that which would have been sufficient.

Let us take as an example the temple No. 3. The diameter of the pillar is $19\frac{5}{7}$ gera, or 2 hath $3\frac{5}{7}$ gera, 7 hath* $3\frac{1}{7}$ gera; amounting in English measurement, omitting some small fractions, to 11 feet 1 inch, or let us say 11 feet. This portion divided between three workmen would give to each a task of $3\frac{2}{3}$ feet at different elevations. In breadth we may suppose each man to operate upon a space of 3 hath, or 3 yards for two men. The extent of the temple No. 3, in the interior, is about 34 hath in width, and 36 in length. Now, according to the task I have allotted to each man, nine would occupy the breadth of the temple, and as each proceeded in his excavations, he would be followed by two others. This calculation gives a line of nine workmen in length and three in depth,

* 1 Hath make 8 gera, 2 Hath make 1 gaz.
1 Gaz ,, 1 yard English, 1 Hath ,, 18 inches.
1 Gera ,, $2\frac{1}{4}$ inches English.

making in all twenty-seven. Let us now add six workmen, two for clearing away and carrying off rubbish. This will make an addition of about ten men. Our estimate will be as follows:

27 stone masons,
10 helpers,
2 smiths to sharpen the chissels,
1 man for sketching the apportioned outline,
—
40 workmen.

Let us now suppose that one man can in two days work through a space of 3 hath in width, 2 hath in height, and 1 in depth; the temple being 36 hath deep, he will have accomplished his task in seventy-two days. Thus the labour of two thousand eight hundred and eighty days would suffice for the excavation of the great hall in the temple, No. 3.

According to this calculation, each workman would excavate daily a space of 20 gera in height, 24 in breadth, and 4 in depth, making 1,920 cubic gera. The entire space excavated would be 7,373,824 cubic gera,* and this without including the chisseling out of the doors and pillars in the interior. Let us now calculate the time expended in sculpturing the ornaments. In these I do not include the statues, I mean simply the arabesques, &c. Let us suppose that each workman sculptures daily 1 hath square of the surface of the wall; according to this calculation the entire would be finished in

* An estimate of the number of cubic gera contained in the temple No. 3:

	Cubic hath.		Cubic gera.
A and B	5 : 4 : 7 . 2	=	280
C	12 : 4 : 7	=	336
D	6 : 7 : 7	=	294
E	7 : 4 : 7	=	196
F	51 : 8 : 7	=	2,856
G and H	8 : 6 : 6 . 2	=	576
I to O	6 : 6 : 6 . 6	=	1,295
F	34 : 36 : 7	=	8,568
			14,402
			512
			7,373,824

five thousand seven hundred and fifty-eight days, not including the time required for the finer touches, and polishing the stone. In this department I should say that two hundred and fifty workmen could be employed at the same time, and could complete their task in twenty-three days. The time occupied in the entire work would be

	Days.
For the excavation of the temple.	4,518
For the finer sculpture work . .	5,758
	10,276

Let us now estimate the expense. The wages, calculated at the present rate of payment, four anas per day, would amount to two thousand five hundred and sixty-nine rupees, a sum far less than one would be inclined to suppose the workmanship of such a temple would cost.

There are other reasons for the slenderness of the cost. There were no materials to be brought from a distance; there was neither mortar nor cement needed, everything was ready to the workman's hand. The number of persons employed in clearing away rubbish, &c. would be very small indeed.

In order to satisfy every doubt, let us suppose that the rock is harder than I calculated, or the workmen less active, or, in short, that I went too far in supposing that each man could excavate daily 1632 cubic inches, let us calculate each workman's toil at half the original estimate, and we have the following result :—

	Days.
For the excavation of the temple.	9,036
For the finer work	5,758
	14,794

Fourteen thousand seven hundred and ninety-four days would entail a cost of three hundred and ninety-three thousand one hundred and seventy-three rupees. This sum is insignificant, considered as payment for the workmanship of such a temple; and appears still more so when contrasted with the expense contracted in the erection of our European dwellings.

I have already remarked that these temples do not, at first sight, impress the beholder with an idea of extraordinary antiquity, but persons looking upon them are apt to believe that they are all of the same age, and were fashioned simultaneously in the living rock. Their extreme antiquity is the cause of this error. The period of their creation is so remote, the mist that time has thrown over them is become in the lapse of ages so dense, that tens and hundreds of years that intervened between the excavating of the different temples, are points rendered by distance too small to fix our attention, and the collective group is presented to the mind as one great whole, the impulse of a single thought, the birth of the same hour.

On a closer inspection of these temples, the difference that we discover in the style of architecture is a sufficient proof that they are not the offspring of the same period of time. The first great distinction observable in in these buildings is that some have flat, others arched roofs. Those with the vaulted roofs are higher, and of a more simple style. The height of the pillars is equal to six diameters, the shaft being plain. Temple No. 14 is in this style. In these temples "the most holy" is never represented by colossal figures. The prevailing symbol is a ball, in which is inserted a handle or spike. If the Temple No. 1 is an exception in being ornamented with a seated Buddha figure, still we find this symbol there, and the great colossal group is placed behind "the most holy," at the point where the two pillared passages that run along either side unite.

The flat-roofed lehnas appear to belong to another period. They are more massive, larger in the interior, and seem to speak of a mystery-loving priesthood wrapping in gloomy shadows a knowledge which the eager eye of the multitude would fain have penetrated.

Here, within these rock-hewn halls, where the foot falls noiseless, within the deep shadow of these massive pillars, and sculptured walls, every thing was disposed so as to produce an impression of awe upon the mind. The sudden appearance of a priest from behind one of the pillars, his abrupt disappearance through one of the side doors, the blaze of light that was sometimes thrown round the chief idol, and again withdrawn, leaving the grim deity wrapped in darkness and in gloom—all this was calculated to produce an effect which could only be experienced in such a place. Even my enemies have never accused me of cowardice, I have never been a ghost-seer, I have never fancied that I was favoured with visions either of giants or fairies, and yet, I must confess that more than once, while exploring these lehnas I have been seized with an involuntary shudder, when on entering a side chamber, or turning suddenly into an angle of the sanctum, my glance has fallen on a colossal and cadaverous human figure, or what appeared to be one. Often, when suddenly looking up from my drawing, or writing, I have been startled by finding one of these giant forms apparently watching me with great intentness, whilst the flickering glare of the torch lent a kind of expression to the countenance, over which it had cast a yellow, corpse-like hue.

Besides the difference discernable in the formation of the roofs, we find others in the internal arrangements of the buildings. In the flat-roofed temples, there are rooms which seem intended for the residence of individuals. These apartments lie contiguous to one another, and seem to have been consecrated to the exercise of the sacred rites of hospitality.

Or, were we to look upon these temples containing apartments as dwellings intended for the priests, and partaking of the character of our cloisters, we should then consider the arch-roofed lehnas destined for a different object, as in them we find no trace of such accommodation.

We find also a great difference in the style of ornament even amongst those that bear the general characteristic of being flat-roofed. Some are very simple, the ornaments of a mythological character, being painted; the others are decorated with the most richly wrought sculpture. The

Lehna No. 14 belongs to the first class, No 1 to the second.

I have already remarked that we do not find in the arch-roofed temples colossal figures placed in the sanctum as objects of veneration, whilst, on the contrary, we invariably find in the flat-roofed lehnas a Buddha figure installed as an object of devotion, or, to speak more correctly, to indicate a spot where the offerings and prayers of the devotees should be presented. Though these figures are to be found in all the flat-roofed temples, they are much more numerous in some than in others.

Taking into consideration this general difference of construction, I should be inclined to look upon the flat-roofed lehnas, containing these sculptured figures, as Buddha temples *par excellence,* furnished with apartments for the priests, and partaking somewhat of the character of our cloisters. They seem to be the work of a later period than the arched-roofed temples, which, from the simplicity of their style, and from their not containing any representation of a Supreme Being in human form, I am inclined to look upon as creations of an elder race. In support of this opinion I may also add, that in these temples, the traces of decay are much more visible than in the others; but whether caused by the hand of time, or the destroying fury of man, I cannot say. The other class of temples with vaulted ceilings, and adorned with sculptured ornaments and figures, I am inclined to look upon as belonging to a more modern period than the former, but still much earlier than the time of the erection of the flat-roofed lehnas. These arch-roofed and ornamented temples were probably the creations of some sects of Buddhists that had separated from the original stock, such as the Faini or others.

I am strongly inclined to believe that these temples are the creations of two distinct sects, differing in their religious views. The difference in the symbolical representations in the sanctum of the two styles of building, confirms me in this opinion. In the arch-roofed temple we have the symbolical form without the human figure, and in the flat-roofed lehna we find the well-known Buddah statues. A difference so great as this cannot be satisfactorily accounted for by supposing that the temples were destined for different uses.

In contemplating the Lehna No. 1, and especially in considering the symbolical stones that ornament the sanctum, I was struck by the similarity between these decorations and those I saw in the Buddha temples in Ceylon and Java. This discovery strengthened the opinion I then formed, that in these temples we find the works of the latest days of Buddhism in India.

In the symbolical stone of Lehna No. 14, we find a simple form, which recurs again, but changed and highly ornamented in Lehna No. 1, where the Buddha figure of the symbolical statue of the Temple No. 15 is incorporated. We have in these symbolical stones, as I shall henceforth name them, a Dagob, beneath which the bones of Buddha are supposed to repose. This form, especially in Lehna No. 14, recalls the Topen or Dopen, as seen in Benares and in Upper India. I am inclined to call these stones, altars, erected over the bones of some person looked upon as very holy, and held up as an object of veneration to others. That such altars should be erected to the memory of Buddha, is very natural. Their form reminds one powerfully of the Lingam, the primitive Indian symbol of fertility produced by the sun, the upper slab or platform representing a place of sacrifice.

The idol in Lehna No. 9, resembles, in simplicity, the symbol in Lehna No. 14. It is a seated Buddha figure, and bears a striking likeness to the Memnon, though the position of the hands is different.

The fourth division of these idols or symbols seems to spring from the symbol in Lehna No. 14. I must, however, admit that this class, as represented in Lehna No. 15, is widely different from the original type. The figure in No. 15 is standing—an attitude that appears extraordinary in a Buddha figure. The whole bearing of the statue, as well as the drapery, reminds me strongly of the colossus at Bamiana.

The upper part of this symbol was too much disfigured to allow me to venture an opinion as to what it might originally have been intended to represent. The time that I spent in Adjinta, I devoted entirely to the inspection of the lehnas, and to sketching and drawing; and I trust that the account contained in these pages, will serve to give a clear idea of these temples. I hope that I shall be pardoned an omission of minor details, as my two days' visit did not allow me to do more than give a general sketch.

I have already frequently alluded to the Lehna No. 1.

The side walls, which are separated from the inner hall by rows of pillars, are decorated with well-executed colossal figures of Buddha. The seat of the symbolical "holiest," is ornamented with a seated figure, and various groups, representing deeds of charity. Above the pillars, between these and the ceiling, is a flat portion of the wall. This is ornamented with a figure of Buddha, sitting on a palang, or bed, and surrounded by several other figures.

The pillars are large and massive, 8 hath high, and 14 gera in diameter.

The Lehna No. 2 is not finished, and the entrance to the pillared portal is half blocked up with rubbish. I measured a broken pillar, and calculated the length of the entire to have been 46 gera in height, and $2\frac{1}{3}$ in diameter. This calculation may be erroneous, as I saw only part of the pillar. It belonged to one of the flat-roofed temples.

The Lehna No. 3 is in an unfinished state, and like No. 2 is flat-roofed. The pillars in the interior are of the height of their diameters.

There are pillars in the interior of the flat-roofed temples, as well as those on the outside. The height of the pillars in the interior is three times their diameter. In the ante-hall the pillars measure $2\frac{1}{2}$ diameters in height. The ornamental work on these pillars is various, the details different in each.

The Lehna No. 4 belongs to the same class as those I have just mentioned. The decorations are more in painting than sculpture. This temple is small, covering a space of only fourteen yards square.

No. 5 resembles No. 3, differing only in some slight particulars. The chief idol is a seated cross-legged figure.

The Lehna No. 6 is like No. 5, the idol of the same kind. In this temple, however, the idol is placed upon a pedestal, on which are sculptured two gazelles, lying before something I did not recognize, and which I do not well know how to describe. I have been assured that it represents a djaku, or discus, which assertion I neither refute nor admit. In the gazelles we unmistakeably recognize that sign in the Indian zodiac corresponding to our twins.

These animals become the more interesting, as on a closer inspection they remind one strongly of the fabled unicorn. I have no intention of writing a chapter on the nearly exhausted theme of mermaids and unicorns, but I think a few words will help to the better understanding of the representation of these animals in the temple. That on the left is intended to be represented with horns and ears, and not with ears only, or the indication of the second horn must be an error on the part of the artist. The gazelle on the left shows no indication of a second horn, and it is very probable that the fable of the unicorn was founded upon representations of this kind, where on a side view, one horn appearing to cover the other, the artist had not thought of indicating the existence of the second.

The pillars in this temple are highly wrought, and though corresponding in general characteristics, are different in detail. Amongst these sculptured ornaments are many female figures, which are always found in abundance in Buddha temples.

The Lehna No. 7 is very like No. 1. The idol is a Buddha figure in a standing posture; the entire is highly ornamented. The interior of the temple resembles No. 15.

The Lehna No. 8 resembles No. 3, but possesses the advantage of being finished. This temple covers a space of 23 square yards, or 46 hath. In the centre is a square, of which the sides are formed by rows of pillars.

The Lehna No. 9 is of the same order of architecture as No 3. It is 50 hath in length, and 52 in breadth. The idol is represented sitting on a low seat; but not cross-legged. The ornaments of this temple, though not particularly interesting, serve as a specimen of the prevaling taste of the people for whom they were executed.

The Lehna No. 10 is covered with rubbish.

The Lehna No. 11 is not completed; but judging by what has been done, the design of the architect seems to have been to fashion this temple in the same style as No. 3, but on a smaller scale. In these lehnas are several small chambers, of which I do not understand the destination. The natives here say they were intended for prisons; but may they not have been apartments for the priests or pupils?

The Lehna No. 12 is like the last-mentioned

temple. There are small chambers surrounding the great square.

The Lehna No. 13 is flat-roofed, rather simple in style, but differing from the others of the same class in the construction of the pillars, which are placed on pedestals of about 1 gera in height. The angles correspond exactly with those of the pillars, so that there is no unevenness.

The Lehna No. 14 is arch-roofed, and of a simple style of architecture. It contains a symbolical stone; but no Buddha figure.

The Lehna No. 15 resembles No. 14, inasmuch as it is arch-roofed; but in execution and decoration it is more like No. 1, whilst the idol resembles that in the Lehna No. 7. The portal of this temple is uninjured, whilst that of No. 14, as well as many pillars in the interior, is demolished.

The Lehna No. 16 is a small temple, with a flat roof. The idol is seated cross-legged in the sanctum, surrounded by standing colossal figures.

The Lehna No. 17 is flat-roofed; but the

arrangement of the pillars differs considerably from that displayed in the temples I have already mentioned. Let us, for example, compare the account of Lehna No. 3 with that of No. 17, and we shall perceive that the sixteen pillars in the centre of the ground floor do not form a square like the twelve pillars of No. 3, but are rather placed in four rows, and lie nearer to the wall. In the upper story the pillars are arranged in the same order as in No. 3, but are supported on a ledge, or raised step, which is not the case in No. 3. In this particular, the Lehna No. 17 resembles No. 13, where the four pillars in the angles are raised on pedestals, 1 gera in height.

The idol is a seated Buddha figure. The door-frames of this temple are highly ornamented.

The under story, or great hall of this temple, encloses a square of 40 hath; the upper story is of the same dimensions.

At the upper end of the second story are three shrines, or apartments containing idols and allegorical figures. In the wall, and facing the great hall, are two niches, in each of which is placed a standing figure.

I do not find anything amongst my papers relative to the Lehna No. 18. If my memory serve me correctly, I think it is one of the smaller temples, and contains nothing deserving of particular notice.

No. 19 is the largest of the flat-roofed temples. The great hall is 97 hath in length, and 70 in breadth. In the hall are twenty-eight pillars, of which the height is four times the diameter.

This temple, which I have observed is the largest of the group, produces a very imposing effect. The idol, a Buddha figure, is gigantic compared to those I saw in the other lehnas. The hands, which are open, measure 2 hath, or 3 English feet in length. Night had stolen upon me whilst taking a survey of the temple; and I ordered some dried grass to be lighted, that I might be able to see what surrounded me.

The Lehna No. 20, like No. 19, is flat-roofed. The artistic skill displayed in the fashioning and ornamenting of this temple is not insignificant: still it will bear no comparison with some of the other temples I have mentioned. My thoughts were solely engrossed by the Lehna No. 19; and even when I had returned to my tent my fancy still wandered through its extensive chambers, and brought back again the colossal statues and lofty walls as I had seen them, rendered still more vast and more mysterious in their aspect by the uncertain light, which sometimes streamed suddenly upwards, sometimes flickered unsteadily from the burning grass.

I am sorry to be obliged to dispute the fame these temples have so long enjoyed, of being gigantic undertakings, in which millions had been expended, and the labours of thousands employed. The general opinion seems now to be that these temples are the offspring of a period, when certain religious sects were persecuted in India; and if we adopt this belief, it will be difficult to suppose that persons so circumstanced could afford a great outlay, either in men or money. Or, did they possess the great power that wealth and numbers give, may we not well suppose that they would rather use it against their persecutors, than employ it in hollowing rocks?

Or, let us suppose that the oldest amongst these temples belong to the time when Buddhism first made its appearance in this part of India, and when its priests, upon their arrival, had chosen this profound retreat as a place where they could in solitude follow the precepts of their religion. The older temples, those executed in the more simple style, may have been excavated at that time; and as Buddhism spread, as the members of its adherents increased, as the congregations became more wealthy as well as more numerous, additional temples may have been hewn out, which showed in their decorations and style of architecture the changes that had taken place in the public taste, and, perhaps in the religious tenets of the sect.

I may here observe that in ancient times, and in Upper India, the followers of Buddhism practised dark and bloody rites, which in after times were rejected, and the ceremonies of the religion took a milder form. The rock-hewn temple at Baniana and the Dopen belong, unmistakeably, to the followers of the ancient rites. Amongst these we may reckon the followers of Schiva, as the use the Dopen and Lingam; and all these symbolical representations, in some way or other, indicate fertility.

The dark tenets of these elder days were succeeded by others of a milder form, the professors of which we may look for in Western India, and who, in all probability, were the artificers of the lehnas of which we have been speaking. This would account for the introduction of the symbolical stone Lingam which we find in the older temples, and for the roughly-hewn Buddha figures, of which the position of the hands indicate fruitfulness and eternity.

The Indian monuments of this period would induce the belief that the inhabitants of the country had then a close intercourse with Ethiopia, or Egypt. Judging from the temples, I should say that Buddhism again underwent a change, or purification: and to this period I would attribute the fashioning of the more elaborately ornamented temples, those in which the symbol of fruitfulness is more dimly visible, and this may have been the time when Buddhism began to spread more extensively through India, and when especially we find traces of it in Bahar. These changes, or purifications in Buddhism, seem to be the germ of those sagas that record his avaters, or incantations.

The many religious wars that arose in Upper India had, no doubt, the effect of urging the followers of Buddhism to the south; and we may find the effects of this fresh influx in the new style of architecture discoverable in the more modern temples, a style that reminds one strongly of the poetical fancy of the disciples of Vishnu, whose followers we probably find in the Jains, or Jyns, though the Jains maintain that they are the root of Buddhism in the south of India, and that the other sects are only branches separated from them. This, of course, the other sects deny, and all are supported by strong arguments. It is probable that a comparison between the architecture of the temples, and the religious rites of the different sects would settle the dispute. I regret that I had not an opportunity of visiting the Jain temples.

CHAPTER XIV.

Departure from Adjinta—Gole ke Gaon—Error arising from the mispronunciation of a word—Selor—Battery—Troublesome servants—Ellora, or Erola—Rosa—Inhabited by Fakirs—Beautiful buildings—Elura—The Kailas—Dilapidated state of some of the buildings—Temples arched and flat-roofed—Influence of the priesthood.

After I had concluded my inspection of the lehnas, I set out in the evening for Gole ke Gaon, where I intended to pass the night; but the mispronunciation of a word deranged my plans. I had confounded Kole Gaon with Gole ke Gaon, and so was obliged to pass the night in a little village, one coss nearer to Adjinta than the place where I had intended to sup. Selor, which lies at a distance of seven coss from Adjinta, was the term of my day's march. To reach it I passed through Leea, Ballodh, and Kamake.

The road was uniform, and led us through an elevated plain. The soil was stony, and covered with low jungle wood. We saw no game of any kind, with the exception of some small antelopes. In Selor there is a bazaar, and, considering the size of the place, a tolerably large population, amongst whom I sought in vain for a turner.

After passing a night in Selor, I resumed my journey, travelled through different villages, and stopped at Aalen. Here I arrived on the day on which the fair or mela was held. This busy scene lasts but one day, and is thronged with purchasers and sellers, who come from a circuit of several miles round.

Battery, the next place at which I stopped, is surrounded by a wall of loam, and, like the generality of the villages here, has very much the appearance of a fortress. In Battery we had an exhibition of dancing-girls, who excelled in tumbling and feats of that kind. This was the first performance of the sort I had seen since I left the Coromandel coast, in which the male performers beat the drum and tambourine.

I have often during my travels in India had occasion to complain of my servants, and I had now again to do with one upon whom remonstrance, entreaties, and representations were alike vain. He persevered coolly and systematically in his evil conduct, and, as one of us could not but submit, I was obliged to yield, at least in secondary things. I have often thought that if I had possessed greater knowledge of the language, so many misunderstandings and quarrels would not have arisen between me and my servants; though, on the other hand, it has sometimes appeared to me that this intractableness was an essential quality in the Indian character, and that their apparent docility arose from a determination to pursue the object they had in view steadily, and unmindful of opposition.

From Battery to Phoolmery the way is three coss long. From Phoolmery the high road leads to Djoka, a distance of two and a half coss. Half a coss farther on is Djaunké; from this place to Alshur is one coss. From the latter village we travelled on to Narungabad, as the natives pronounce it, or, as others call it, Aurungabad. I did not choose this route, for Ellora, the object of my long-formed wishes, lay a different way.

The distance from Phoolmery to Ellora, or, as it is here called, Erola, by not passing through Aurungabad, is as follows: Three coss to Wary Gaon, two coss thence to Sultanpoor, two coss more to Gadana, thence one coss to Bharji, another coss to Rossa, and then one coss to Erola, making in all eleven coss from Phoolmery to Erola.

From Battery to Wary Gaon, where my tent was prepared, is a distance of five coss. Wary Gaon is a comfortable-looking village. After leaving Phoolmery, the aspect of the country improved, particularly when contrasted with the last day's march, during which all had been so dreary. But now a smiling landscape, similar to that which I had left in Hindoostan, again presented itself, and luxurious gardens and lovely plaintain trees, and fertile fields and meadows again offered themselves to the eye. Still agriculture has not made much progress in the country. Some persons have assured me that this is owing to the want of a proper currency being established in the district; and in support of this argument, added that it would be very difficult to get pais (a small copper coin) at the bazaar, if one, in purchasing, gave a larger piece, out of which some money ought to be returned. This I was inclined to look upon rather as a proof of the unwillingness of the vendors to deal honestly with the purchasers.

I dispatched some of my servants from Wary Gaon to Elora, with directions to arrange my camp there. When, however, I arrived in Rosa, a place formerly adorned by Aurungzib with mosques and mausoleums, I found that my people had thought well of fixing my quarters there. Rosa may be called a colony of fakirs; the entire population is Mahomedan, and to this circumstance I may attribute the fact of my tent being erected there. My Hindoo munschis, who had been hitherto at the head of my establishment, had lately left me, and the office of comptroller of my household had been since filled by an old Mahomedan, who had been travelling with me for the last two years, and who of course exercised considerable influence over my suite. On this account, as long as I did not personally interfere, the Moslems in my retinue had a majority; and Rosa was in their eyes a place rendered sacred by being the abode of so many pious fakirs, and the spot where the bones of so many of the saints of their faith reposed, whilst Elura, the work of the unbelieving Hindoos, was an object of execration to them.

Rosa must once have been very handsome, and in looking upon its majestic gateways, mosques, and mausoleums, one is tempted to believe that Aurungzib, or whoever imitated him here, was desirous that the Mahomedan buildings at Rosa should excel the Hindoo works at Elura.

I felt no pleasurable emotion, no glow of enthusiasm, in contemplating the buildings at Rosa. The recollection of the hypocritical and fanatical monster who had adorned the place, cooled my imagination. I remained some hours in an old mosque, which was used as a bungalow, and waitd until my tent was erected in the great temple at Elura, a spot which I had chosen in the morning.

I may, *en passant*, remark, that the monuments and buildings of Rosa are, in general, of beautifully-wrought white marble. The mausoleums of the imperial family are especially distinguished by their beauty ; but the inspection of these, as well as a visit to the highly-venerated graves of some departed fakirs, was denied by the guardian priests, although they took a deep interest in the income arising from such visits.

Elula,* or Elura, is about half a coss from Rosa, and lies at the foot of the mountain, on the summit of which Rosa is situated. The rock is of the same kind as that of the mountain at Adjinta, in which the lehnas are wrought.

* This difference in the orthography is striking enough. The natives in general call the place Erula, some few say Ellora. I am like a traveller who stands doubtingly at a cross-road: though unwilling to abandon the sweet-sounding Ellora, still to avoid disputes, by yielding something to both sides, I am willing to write the name Elura.

The temples of Elura cannot boast the number of beautiful trees, which adorn those of Rosa; still they are not wholly destitute of the protection of these "green-robed senators." Immediately before the great temple of Kailas is a large tree, within the shade of which I ordered my tent to be pitched.

Descending the road from Rosa, a wide way, on which one meets many beasts of burden, and before reaching the foot of the mountain, we find, on the right-hand side of the road, a right-angled excavation, within which stands the temple of Kailas, not only hollowed in the rock, but also distinctly cut out from the mountain. One could step from the road on to the roof of the temple.

Of the temple of Elura I shall speak here only in general terms. From the foot of the mountain range, in which the temples of Elura lie, a wide plain is spread before the eye, extending, the natives say, to the sea-coast.

The temple of Kailas is the middle point of the row of temples at Elura. On the south lie many of these rock-hewn edifices, of a simple style of architecture; on the north are many smaller, but more artistically wrought.

I spent fourteen days at Elura, occupied from morning until evening in measuring and making drawings in the temples. When the waning light no longer permitted me to continue my occupations, I wandered through the mountain, visiting temples that I had not yet seen; nor did I ever think of dining until darkness shrouding the landscape, shut every object from my view, and I was obliged to return to my tent. During this time, I found every day temples that had not yet been visited; and I am convinced that travellers coming after me will frequently discover many that have not yet been mentioned.

None of these temples show traces of demolition occurring in modern times, with the exception of some of the Buddha temples of the more simple style, lying to the south of the Kailas. In these, the *façade* of the temple was broken away, and many of the pillars in the interior overthrown. It may, however, be questioned whether these signs of destruction have been produced by the hand of the Mussulman or by the agency of nature—whether this demolition arose from the ordinary natural processes, or whether some especial shock produced the catastrophe.

If we suppose the work of destruction to be accomplished by man, our suspicions naturally fall on the Moslems. But then the question arises, why these temples in particular should have been singled out, and others, containing a far greater number of figures, be allowed to pass unnoticed? This objection is particularly applicable to the temple of Kailas, which being the most conspicuous of all, and lying directly in the way from Rosa, might naturally be supposed to attract the first ebullition of the enemy's fury. These arguments, I feel, are not fully satisfactory, as we must admit that the will of the destroyers was the only rule which they needed to follow; still, it seems remarkable that those temples which were most remote should have suffered, and that the others, which appear more likely to have awakened the wrath of the versary, were passed unnoticed; or, still supposing that the injury sustained by the temples was the work of man, may we not be justified in attributing it to some of the followers of Brahma? And, adopting this opinion, we may very well believe that these sectarians, instead of defacing, would only alter the decorations of the temples in some degree, and adapt the building to the celebration of their own religious rites. It also appears highly probable that the changes wrought in these temples are solely the work of time, effected by the weather, wearing away by the action of water, or the accidental falling of masses of rock.

Were we to adopt the opinion that an earthquake had been the agent of destruction, we must admit it to have been a very partial one indeed. The broken pillars, lying in some of the temples, can scarcely be looked upon as proofs of religious persecution, for it is much more probable that religious bigots would destroy the idols and decorations than the pillars; and a broken arm or a defaced nose is the greatest disfigurement that the stone deities have endured, which is nothing more than their brethren in all the temples of India have to complain of—if they could.

I will conclude my remarks on this subject by saying that those temples which have suffered most are the oldest of the group. These all lie to the south of Kailas, and have evidently belonged to the followers of Buddha. Those on the north are of a more modern date, and amongst them the Thumal is conspicuous.

The history of the temples of Elura, as far as regards the date of their formation, and the names of the artificers, is wrapped in darkness. The difference, however, in structure and decoration shows clearly that this group of temples was not the work of one religious sect.

In speaking of the lehnas at Adjinta, I classed them into flat and arch-roofed. A distinction may also be made in the temples of Elura, between which and those of Adjinta a great similarity of form exists. In both, the colossal Buddha figure is to be seen; but there are no arch-roofed temples in Elura, and consequently the symbolical stone Dagob is wanting. We find in Elura, independently of Kailas, temples of which the roofs are flat. The temples are adorned with the richest sculptures, and, one may almost say, overstocked with shrines. In the lehnas of Adjinta all the objects of veneration are concentrated in one point, whilst in Elura the idols are placed along each wall.

Besides the large temples, we find a great number of small ones, all evidently designed as places of worship, and furnished with well-carved symbolic figures. There are others of a different character, in which the decorations represent scenes from the Indian mythology. This dissimilarity seems to me to furnish good grounds for supposing that these temples were the work of various sects, differing more or less from each other in their religious tenets.

We find the priests in every nation very anxious to promulgate their own particular doctrines, and ever zealous to promote works that will tend to give their own religious tenets a preponderance in the nation. In the furtherance of these views, they are not always willing to put their hands into their own pockets, and their ingenuity in finding out ways of working on the credulity of their adherents is marvellous. That this system should have prevailed in India, where superstition was so rampant, may be readily believed, and the payment of the expenses incurred in fashioning a temple for the celebration of religious rites might be naturally regarded as a very meritorious work. Under these circumstances, we may suppose these temples to have been the work of wealthy individuals, who were willing thus to purchase for themselves, under the direction of the priests, an abode in Paradise, whilst, from their contemporaries, they would receive that praise so flattering to self-love, and enjoy the proud consciousness that their works would astonish after ages.

CHAPTER XV.

Comparison between the Indian and Egyptian buildings—Greater labour expended on the Egyptian edifices—Design of the Indian temples—A Brahmin and priest attached to the Kailas—Buddha temple on the roof of the Kailas—Surmises suggested by this discovery—Flatterers preferable to rough boors—A last look at the Kailas—Temples in the side walls—Departure from Elura—Lassar—Bayjapoor—Murder of a Radjput—Departure from Bayjapoor.

Many persons, in speaking of the gigantic works of the ancient inhabitants of India, declare that they eclipse those of the Egyptians. For my own part, I must confess that I am a warm admirer of the people of India, both ancient and modern, and would be sorry to detract from their fame; but I must candidly say that the works of Indian architecture, gigantic though they be, cannot, with justice, be pŭt in comparison with those of the master-minds of Egypt.

In the first place, the Egyptians had very great difficulties to contend with in the erection of their buildings, which were, besides, attended with very great expense. In contemplating works of this kind, a knowledge of the difficulties overcome, and the patience displayed in surmounting them, heightens the admiration of the beholder. The perseverance of the Egyptian architect was largely taxed, and the accounts that Herodotus has left of roads laid down and dams erected, prove that these buildings are not alone admirable for their vastness, but become stupendous when taken in connection with the immense amount of labour expended on them.

If we only consider the pyramid of Cheops, the distance from which the stones must have been brought, and the mechanical power needed to raise them to their destined height, we are amazed at the accomplishment of such designs. Then the construction of Lake Meros, 3,600 stadii in circumference, and two pyramids, each 600 feet high, rising from the centre, and the labyrinth with its three thousand chambers. The difficulties overcome in the construction of these buildings place them, beyond all comparison, beyond the rock temples of India. The stones for the Egyptian works must have been first hewn and polished, which entailed considerable expense, whilst in India, as I before remarked, the materials were all ready to the workman's hand, and the rubbish and broken parts easily got rid of by being swept over the projecting rock.

I freely admit that the design of the Indian temples seems to me grander than that discoverable in the Egyptian buildings. The plan of the Kailas, I call a gigantic thought; and the imposing effect which the great rock-hewn hall produced upon me, at first sight, was never weakened during the many days that I devoted entirely to the contemplation of that majestic work—the embodiment of a grand idea, transmitted from by-gone ages. The temple of Thumal, lying to the north of the Kailas, is equally grand; nor can anything at Elephanta, or Salsette, be compared with these superb works.

The temple of Thumal is one of the greatest wonders of Elura. Rows of colossal pillars extend to a distance that seems illimitable. Advancing through these pillared aisles, and turning to the right, we find ourselves in an enclosure, arched in by the blue sky, whilst beneath our feet lies a vast reservoir, to which there appears no other access than the steps we have just descended. One feels as if suddenly placed within the deep bosom of the great mountain, but looking up, we see the same sky, the same sun that we left without, shining far, far above the rocky sides of the profound enclosure. On the other side of the temple, and exactly opposite to this outlet, an excavation admits the light through a vast mass of rock in the same manner. Here, as on the opposite side, we find a reservoir, smaller than the former, and which appears to have been intended for the use of the inhabitants of the temple.

Having finished our inspection of the temples

of Elura, we will now pass to those situated in the plain. These are inhabited, and used for the celebration of religious rites. To these temples is also given the name of Elura, or, to gratify the Brahmins, for once let us say Erula. They are evidently very old, and would awaken a warm interest, did not their vicinity to the rock-temples place them in humiliating contrast with those Titan palaces. The temples in the plain are surrounded with handsome trees and a few houses, belonging, for the most part, to Brahmin families.

The rock-temples of Elura are forsaken by priests and votaries. I found, however, in the Kailas an old Indian recluse, who told me that he was successor to another of the same class. He had chosen the great hall of the handsomest temple for his abode, and disfigured it with an extensive outlay of mud-mortar, with which he had constructed a kitchen, an elevated seat, and a sleeping place. His selection of a dwelling had not been prompted so much by the beauty of the place, as by the consideration that the Kailas was frequented by great numbers of visitors, whose gifts constituted his income.

He called himself the guardian of the temple, but, except in what immediately concerned himself, he seemed to regard the entire structure with wonderful indifference.

Besides this Brahmin, who had established himself in the Kailas, a priest, from one of the temples in the plain, came every day to perform the purifications or water-sprinkling, and to offer flowers before the idol. This idol, a Schivast stone, was very well attended, no day passed on which the prescribed formalities were not performed; and the priest told me that he had been appointed to this office by the English government, and received a small salary for his services. How far this assertion may be true, I cannot say. I have heard similar things said in various parts of India. Whether in the present case my informant hoped to move me to the bestowing of a larger gift by a statement of his dignity, I know not, but certainly a knowledge of the honour he enjoyed had no weight with me, nor did it induce me to add one fraction to the gratuity I presented to him, and the dweller in the temple. But my present, I believe, far exceeded their expectations, for they both became my most devoted servants. Every command that I gave was declared to be just, and trees were felled and bushes cleared away without an objection being made, or a doubt raised as to whether these orders would entail injury or detract from the beauty of the place. I was allowed to rule and order as I pleased, and whatever I did was declared to be excellent.

I learned here that one of the Buddha temples north of the Kailas had been some time before inhabited by an old Indian, but not finding his income equal to his expectations, he had changed his abode, and sought a more promising retreat.

On the morning of my departure from Elura, I ascended the roof of the Kailas, and found there, amongst the carvings with which the highest point of the building is decorated, a relievo, representing a seated figure with raised hands. It was evidently the work of a Buddhist, and seemed to represent a person in prayer. This fact may give rise to a variety of opinions, and persons who are disposed to look upon the rock-temples as works wrought by the followers of Buddha, might find in this relievo a support for their arguments, and a proof that even the Kailas—the erection of which has never yet been disputed with the Mahomedans—was a Buddha structure, and altered by the Moslems.

To adopt such an opinion would be running a great risk. For my part, I should more readily believe that I had been mistaken in supposing the relievo to represent a Buddha figure, than that the entire temple could have undergone so great a change. Is it not possible that there might have been amongst the numerous workmen engaged in adorning the building a Buddhist, who indulged his own feelings in carving this relievo? though how such an innovation could escape the eye of the overseeing architect cannot be easily accounted for.

I have always detested sycophants, but in ascending the Kailas, a little incident occurred which made me think that it is much more agreeable to come in contact with soft-tongued flatterers than with uncultivated boors. In clambering up the stony way, I was assisted by one of my servants. As the difficulties increased, I asked him whether he was strong enough to carry me. He immediately replied: "I am strong, and he who eats my lord's bread has good reason to be so." I formed a good opinion of him on the spot, and retain it still. I should consider myself a fool did I not prefer the pliant flatterer Glasy to the boorish Umrau, a young bearer, whom, since the affair in the Himalaya, where he was unjustly suspected of having abstracted some money, I had always treated with particular indulgence, and who, notwithstanding, gave me incessant cause for complaint.

Before leaving Elura, I paused to cast a last lingering look upon the Kailas; nor can I forbear adding here a few words more upon this architectural wonder. I have already said that the temple stands out distinct from the rock, which forms thus, on three sides of the building, a great perpendicular wall. Within this wall, on the three sides, are excavations, forming small temples or halls. Steps lead to these rock-hewn dwellings, and the entire is connected by galleries. On the left, or north side, of the Kailas, is a flight of steps, in good preservation, leading to a large temple excavated in the mountain, lighted and ventilated through a great colonnade.

This temple is one of the handsomest in the side walls, all of which form, with the Kailas, a great whole, formerly connected by a bridge hewn out of the solid rock, and of which traces still remain. Many European works speak of this bridge as still existing, but fragments alone lie scattered about. That the destruction of the bridge belongs to a time which, compared with the great age of the temples, may be called modern, seems very probable.

Having left Elura, I directed my way towards Lassar, a tolerably large village, situated on a narrow river, in which, at present at least, the quantity of water is very small, though from morning until evening women are to be seen there washing and bathing.

During the first part of the way, the country was very charming; the road near Elura level, or rather sloping towards the valley, which lay between two mountains. The mist that hovered in the distance warned us that we were approaching the coast; and I fancied that

I already inhaled the sea-air—an odour for which I have little relish.

During my stay at Elura, grapes had every day appeared on my table, which I looked on as a very ordinary circumstance. I was too closely busied with the lehnas to give much attention to such things; but on leaving Elura I was very much surprised to learn that grapes were a rarity in the district, and to be found only in a few villages. The majority of the inhabitants are Hindoos.

My next resting-place was Bayjapoor, which lies at a distance of nine coss from Lassar. I was here waited on by a numerous deputation of the Hindoo inhabitants, praying my assistance under very distressing circumstances. It happened that a few days before, during the solemnity of the Moharrum, that a Radjput, an inhabitant of the place, went out two hours before sunset to fetch some fire. Four Moslems—two of them inhabitants of Bayjapoor—met him, and drawing their dalwars, rushed on him. The contest was unequal, the Radjput was murdered. The mother of the deceased was living. He had also left a brother aged fifteen. The family was poor, and none of them had ever been known to do anything that could give a pretext for the manifestation of such enmity. Some persons looked upon the act as a retaliation for the murder of two Mussulmen who, eight years before, during the Moharrum, had met their death at the hands of the Hindoos of Bayjapoor.

As may be naturally supposed, I could give no assistance in such a case. The man was dead, and it would have been very unbecoming in a private individual, passing accidentally through a town, to take the administration of justice into his hands, though such is the state of things in that part of the country, that I might easily have taken upon myself the part of judge in the affair.

I advised that the body should be buried, which the friends of the deceased, thirsting for vengeance, had hitherto delayed doing. I also recommended that the bazaar should be opened. This advice was of too pacific a nature to be acceptable. I was inclined to believe that the whole affair, particularly as far as the Moslems were concerned, was an outburst of sectarian animosity.

The village magistrate was a Brahmin, but he was under the jurisdiction of a Mussulman resident in Nauringabad, who was himself controlled by Tagirdars, who abode in Hyderabad. The way to the chief justice was thus blockaded. I know that in Bengal or Hindoostan the case would have been different, as the English authorities would have interfered; but here the administration of justice is vested in the hands of the natives.

Though the death of the Radjput was ascribed to animosity arising from a difference of opinion in matters of religion, the toleration of the Indians upon such subjects is well known. The Hindoos, in particular, are tolerant in regard to the religious opinions of their neighbours. It is, indeed, undeniable that some persons in power have profited by the difference of opinion existing between the various sects in India, to awaken a feeling of animosity which they turn to their private advantage; and in the case of the Radjput's death a couple of hundred rupees would have silenced the cries for vengeance. Persons acquainted with Indian intrigues will easily undertand this; everything is made a pretext for extorting money.

Bayjapoor and the district around are under the jurisdiction of a sahab, or bharra sahab, who resides in Hyderabad, and is himself a delegate of the nabob of that place. The Hindoos importuned me to give them a few lines to the resident at Hyderabad, corroborating their statement, as they feared that otherwise, after taking the trouble of going there, they might be sent back unsatisfied. I could not refuse this request. I was only asked to testify to what I had seen. I gave the document they wished for, which amounted to no more than that I had seen a Radjput lying dead, and that his death seemed to have been caused by violence. There were numbers of witnesses, who could give more accurate information, but what I had written was considered so important, that a deputation was appointed to carry it to Hyderabad. As the preparations for this embassy would cause some delay, I have no doubt that in the mean time the payment of a few hundred rupees gave the proceedings a more pacific character.

Numbers of the Hindoo Radjputs crowded every day about my tent. The beauty of these people was striking.

I left Bayjapoor, and after a march of nine coss, through an uncultivated country, enlivened by the occasional appearance of some antelopes, I arrived at the village, or, as it is here called, City of Feola. From the aspect of the place, it did not seem to me very important; the inhabitants, however, entertain a very different opinion, and boasted of their city being governed by a sirdar, whose name I have forgotten.

CHAPTER XVI.

Sirdar of Feola's Fortress—Visit from a strange old man—Fancies himself a pensioner of the company—My baggage is missed—Strange freak of my horse—A visit from a fakir and his tigers—Method of discovering a tiger's lair—Nasak—Rock temples—Inscriptions — Departure from Nasak—Gonda — Circuitous route—Lovely mountains—Recollections of childhood—Arrow-seed.

Six coss to the north of Feola lies the fortress of the mighty sirdar, of whom I had heard so much. It is built upon a mountain, and commands a view of the country round. The fortress is now abandoned, six sepoys being left to guard a single cannon; all that the English thought worth leaving, and even this is spiked. It is said that, in former times, if war raged in the district, the inhabitants took refuge in this fortress, which, I have been told, is large enough to afford shelter to several thousand persons.

I received a visit from one of the wealthy inhabitants of the place. He was an old man, and expressed a strong desire that I should write down his name. He gave many wise reasons for his wish to see his name recorded in my journal. I began to think he was a fool, and was quite confirmed in the opinion when he told me that the Company allowed a pension to all the respectable inhabitants of the town; that, for his part, he received twelve hundred rupees yearly, for which no service was required in return. As the man was neither one of the petty princes of the country who had sold their inheritance to the Company, nor one whose aid could be of any importance, I did not know in what light to regard his story. It is probable that he mistakes his position, and whilst enjoying his patrimonial inheritance, finds a pleasure in fancying himself the Company's pensioner. I wrote down his name in my tablets, which seemed to afford him great satisfaction.

I reached Nebal, under a noonday sun. I had been told that the distance from Feola to Nebal was twelve coss. This was one of the most disagreeable marches I had ever made. To add to my annoyance, my luggage had not arrived. Inquiries were made on the high road and on bye roads that joined the main branch. All was useless; the luggage could not be found. The general opinion was that it had been carried off by the Bhiels, and as our guide belonged to that class, the opinion seemed to be well-grounded.

This was not a very agreeable idea, but my attention was turned away from the uncomfortable suspicion by a reality, which was not a whit more consoling. Riding along the road, ruminating on the probable fate of my luggage, I allowed my horse to choose his own way, and go at the pace he pleased. It suddenly occurred to me that I ought to compel him to assume a more stately bearing. The animal was about five years of age, sure-footed and strong-limbed, as the mountain breed usually are. I had bought him on the Pir Penjal a year and a half before, and had been always well pleased with him. I now gave him the spur, and worked the bit in his mouth. This happened at a spot surrounded by brushwood, not far from a sudden turn in the road, which I had not before observed. Not satisfied with the docility of my horse, I applied the whip, and he started off at full gallop head foremost. The next instant I saw the bed of a river lying directly in the way before me.

Too much vexed to care much about the chance of an accident, I thought, like the boy whose hands were benumbed, "my horse has a fancy for falling:" and though there was still time to save myself from the precipice, I neglected to profit by it, and my horse, unmindful of the spur, plunged thoughtlessly forward, nor perceived his danger until the fore part of his body was already hanging over the abyss. He made a momentary effort to check himself, but in vain, and both horse and rider tumbled down the declivity.

The dry bed of the river was filled with large gravel, which was less hurtful than stones would have been. I escaped with some bruises.

The village is small, and though I had been

told the day before that a fajirdar abode there, I found this intelligence false. The place belongs to the English, and is dependant on the Bombay presidency.

A fakir visited me, accompanied by two leopards, a tiger, and a bear. These, according to his account, had been inhabitants of the mountain range which lay to the north. In the neighbourhood is a river which the natives consider large, but which at that time contained very little water. It is called Kado.

According to the general rumour, this place is frequented by tigers, as is also the mountain district lying near Elura. A zemindar who resided at the distance of some coss from Elura, has often assured me of this, and added that English officers came into the neighbourhood tiger shooting, upon which occasions he had been useful to them.

The mode in which the hunters proceeded was to fasten some animal, a cow, goat, or sheep, in the neighbourhood of the place where the tiger was supposed to have his lair. The spot in which the bait was fastened was selected under some protecting rock, and the peculiar construction of the mountain ridge, affords numberless facilities of this kind. The bait was exposed over night, and if, on the following morning, it was found that the poor sheep or goat had been carried off or killed, an immediate search was instituted. If the tiger were discovered, or roused from his lair, the huntsmen fired from the rock, where they stood in safety. In this case, the tiger could scarcely escape.

The zemindar said that he generally received a present of a couple of rupees, and had besides the prize money promised by the English government to any one who shot a tiger. He gave the further pleasing information, that there were then in the neighbourhood a couple of large tigers, who had carried off a couple of his flock, and that he could almost point out the spot where they were lurking, and if I were disposed to enjoy a tiger-hunt, he offered to expose a couple of small animals during the night.

This happened during the time I passed at Elura, and though so absorbed in the lehnas, I could not resist the temptation that a tiger-hunt offered. I therefore ordered the zemindar to expose a couple of his flock at my expense, but several days passed over, and no tiger appeared, the sheep remained unhurt, and the zemindar and I were disappointed. I bore my share in the disappointment better than I otherwise should have done, as the lehnas engrossed my mind so absolutely, that even the chase lost something of its wonted interest.

Having left Nebal, or Nebar, a march of thirteen coss brought me to the large town of Nasak or Nasik. This place is beautifully situated, and is surrounded by gardens, planted with mangoe trees. When from a distance, I beheld this beautifully shaded town, I fixed the spot on which I wished my tent to be placed; but when I arrived, I looked around in vain for my wide-striped, blue and white, petchooba.

The prospect of being left tentless was not at all pleasant, and I wandered in search of my petchooba through all the streets of the town. In my rambles, I had an opportunity of seeing the bathing places, and some fine old temples well wrought in massive stone. I was told of a rajah who lives in this place, and who has an Englishman in his house, in quality of teacher. Whether this tutor was one of the rajah's choice, or whether he had been appointed by the government, I could not learn.

I found neither the temples nor the other antiquities of the place worthy of particular attention, but I must say of Nasak, that of all the Indian towns, it is that in which I saw the prettiest maidens, and the handsomest carving in wood. I know not what opinion the reader may form of my negligence, but I must confess that I did not seek to make an intimate acquaintance with the former, nor did I make drawings of the latter.

In the middle of the town, there is a large building, the curtwali, or town-house, in which the resident sub-collector holds his office, and where he attends on the days that business requires his presence.

Having rested one day at Nasak, I set off for the mountains in which the temples are wrought. These temples are commonly known as the lehnas of Nasak. The number of these structures amounts to about twenty, but to any one who has seen the mighty works of Elura, they will scarcely seem worth the trouble of a visit.

They are incontestably the work of Buddhists, and the decorations, in many parts, reminded me strongly of what I had seen at Elura. Amongst them were the lotus-branches, or stalks, interwoven round the arched gateways. The workmanship is rude, and some are of opinion that these temples are of an earlier date than those of Elura. For my part, I am inclined to regard them as the work of a small and poor congregation, cut off by circumstances from those who had made greater progress in the fine arts than they.

I am inclined to believe that many of these structures were intended for dwellings, rather than for temples. Even the large lehnas, with the exception of those with arched roofs, were, I think, intended as abodes for a confraternity. One may form the same opinion of the rock-temples of Adjinta, looking upon the flat-roofed as dwellings for the priests, and regarding the arch-roofed lehnas as the actual temples. It will be, however, difficult to reconcile this hypothesis with the fact, that we find idols in the temples of both styles of structure, unless we look upon these seated Buddha figures as placed in the temples of the second order to satisfy the private devotion of the dwellers in these abodes. Again it may be asked why we do not find a dagob in any of the temples at Adjinta, and again, why this seated Buddha figure is installed in the temples of Elura, as the chief object of veneration, if the entire aspect of the structure did not give reason to suppose that these temples were intended as habitations for the priests.

In the floor of the lehnas of Nasak, are stones, raised about four or five inches above the level of the ground. These stones were used for grinding corn, but are now so worn away in many places, that instead of being elevations they form indentures. In the angles of the doors and windows of one of the larger temples, there is projecting fret-work, evidently an addition made long after the lehna had been completed, and intended evidently as grooves for wooden frames. Some accidental circumstances might have rendered such a precaution necessary for the safety of the inmates.

The mountain in which these lehnas are hollowed out, stands alone in the midst of the valley. The temples occupy about two thirds of the mountain in height, and extend all round. I did not visit those on the west side, which were represented to me as insignificant, and not containing anything worth seeing. The springs were abundant, and in every temple there was a small reservoir.

If the lehnas of Nasak did not attract my admiration by their vastness, I must in justice say that, though not comparable to those of Elura, the ornaments and figures were well carved. I found in these temples, pehlevi, or inscriptions, which awakened a lively interest in my mind. They were the first that I had seen in these rock-temples of the north of India.

I found another inscription in one of the small temples, or dwellings, whichever it may be, of the lehnas. It was carved upon a pillar, which still remained upright, though all around was in ruins. This inscription was placed so high as to be beyond the reach of a man's arm. The discovery of these inscriptions gives me reason to hope that the age of the temples may yet be discovered.

Having finished my inspection of the lehnas

of Nasak, I proceeded on my way towards the village of Gonda, where I had ordered my tent to be pitched. There is no bungalow here for travellers. The country is, for the most part, uncultivated, and the zemindars seem to have no other commodity to bring to market than dried grass, of which I met several loads on the road. I also saw great quantities cut down, and arranged in heaps, as I passed along the foot of the mountain.

The distant mountain chains, of which I caught a view as I passed, were highly picturesque in form. I do not remember to have seen anything like them. I met a great number of Panjaros on the road, some coming towards me, others journeying in the same direction as myself. Amongst these I remarked one woman, whose arm from the wrist to the elbow was covered with bracelets, some made of glass, others of bronze or silver. The arm was dreadfully swollen and disfigured from the pressure of these rings, but what will not female vanity endure! Let the ornaments remain, the hand may go to perdition, if it cannot accommodate itself to the taste of the wearer.

Leaving Gonda, I made a long day's march of what might have been a short one. Attracted by the unusual appearance of a mountain range, lying towards the north, I left the direct road, and took my course in that direction. I passed through Bodely. One coss farther on, I reached Wakera. Pursuing my journey, I passed several villages, some lying directly in my path, others to the right, some to the left, until I at length arrived at the foot of the mountains. To reach this point, I had been obliged to cross a river. Turning now to the south, I arrived at the village of Bibelgaow; and still journeying along the mountain foot, I came to the village of Ekadpur at two o'clock in the afternoon, having left Gonda at break of day.

If the beautiful contour of the mountains had, at a distance, attracted my admiration, a close view afforded me still greater enjoyment, and amply idemnified me for the wearisome march by which I had reached them. The sides, clothed with a rich vegetation, and many a field that gave promise of an abundant harvest, presented a delightful prospect.

The beautiful trees which surrounded the villages, and concealed many a straw-roofed hut, tended considerably to the embellishment of the scenery; and the foot of the mountain covered with dark brushwood, formed an agreeable contrast with the grassy summit. With the green, sweet-smelling underwood was mixed the Chinese shrub, with its red blossoms. This reminded me of the days of my childhood, when I used to think red and yellow trees would have more richly ornamented the earth than simple green. But now, when I looked at the leafless branches of the Chinese shrub, covered to the very point with red blossoms, I again and again repeated that, whatever might be their beauty, they never could be compared to the soft green, in all its beautiful varieties of shade.

The inhabitants of the villages about Nasak do not speak Hindoostanee, which made it very difficult for me to establish a communication with them. About two coss from Bibelgaon, I passed by the village of Vajungaon, of which I made a drawing. It lies beneath the projecting brow of Mount Gurun-ka-bahar, at the foot of which the river Bhamnatty springs forth. When I saw it, the bed was nearly dry, but in the rainy season there is abundance of water.

I heard nothing in this neighbourhood of lehnas or rock-temples, and found it very difficult to explain myself on this subject with the natives, all of whom were profoundly ignorant of Hindoostanee, nor did my servants fare better.

I am inclined to think that a search for lehnas would not be useless here. The neighbourhood is fruitful, and the mountains in every respect very like those in which the temples of Adjinta, Elura, and Nasak are excavated. This leads me to think that similar works might be found here. If the country about is uncultivated, that is rather to be ascribed to the scantiness of the population than to the barrenness of the soil.

I inquired for arrow-reed, and was told that in this neighbourhood karmuty-wood is used for making these weapons. I was further informed that this wood was selected for the purpose, because it possesses the peculiarity of splitting whilst flying, if the point be previously bitten, in consequence of which, three or sometimes five wounds are inflicted by a single arrow.

Ekadpur. Water boils at 207,3000′. I was well assured of this, before I could give it credence. I left the bungalow, which was occupied by an engineer, his attendants, and a numerous company of females, and proceeded on my way to the ghat, a distance of about one coss. This journey could have been quickly performed, but the engineer, possibly to break the monotony of the way, had so laid down the line of road, that at every hundred paces we met an ascent, then a descent, at the foot of which a new eminence arose, and thus was our patience exercised through the entire way. The route from the ghat to Maw presents an agreeable contrast, and is a handsome specimen of the public works in the Bombay presidency.

The aspect of the mountains, richly clothed with trees and underwood, is delightful to the eye. We found little cottages along the way, separated from one another by a distance of one coss, sometimes of two. In one of these, as well as in the bungalow, there were suwars from Poona stationed on police duty. The grass, through nearly the entire way, was burned down. Advancing through the plain towards Bombay, gracefully formed mountains rose to view along the southern bounds of the horizon, and sometimes, though not so frequently, we caught a glimpse of mountains to the north.

Poona is reckoned two days' march from the bungalow of Kassera. Kallumgaon is three coss from the bungalow of Karly. In Kallumgaon, I saw a cocoon, a kind of silk-worm, which excited my curiosity. It was in the hand of a woodman, who told me that these cocoons were used for tying the barrels of guns to the stocks, for which purpose they were well suited, being stronger than sinews. These cocoons are also used to stop the ends of the bamboo canes, which filled with wooden tinder, serve as lights. For this purpose one end of the cocoon is cut off, and the remainder fits on like a thimble. These cocoons are accumulated by the insect on the branches of the high trees, and so fall into the hands of the woodmen. For a small present, the man gave me the cocoon, which I wished to add to my collection; but I never found an opportunity of getting any information about the insect or butterfly to which it belonged.

Kallumgaon. Water boiled at a temperature 209⅔, 1400′. Kallumgaon signifies literally writing-reed village. There must have been some reason for this appellation, but though I found many different species of reed here, I did not see any of those which are used for writing.

I pursued my way, and having travelled six coss, arrived at my little encampment. The country is, on the whole, very like Ekadpur, but that there are fewer mountains, and the way is less steep. We passed Khurgaon, where a regiment belonging to the Company was stationed. It was four hundred men strong, and was destined to commence a campaign against the Bhiels.

The woods along which we had passed for several days, were all of the same character. No game—even parrots were scarce; indeed, since we left the bungalow, I had seen but two, and these appeared to be deserters flying from the general corps.

In Barka, the cultivation of the land is less attended to. The streets are filled with Panjaras and their oxen, harnessed to hoeckerys, oxen waggons filled with merchants' wares.

CHAPTER XVII.

Approach to Bombay—My camel drivers desert—Application to a magistrate—Drinking-houses—Arrival in Parcil—Thoughts of returning to civilized life—Politeness of Sir George Arthur—Elephanta—Salsette—The Parsees of Bombay—Personal beauty of the men and women—An evening passed in a Parsee family—Comparison between the beauty of the English and Indian ladies—My object in writing this book.

Bombay is reckoned twenty coss from Barka. The nearer we approached the city, the more wretched an appearance did the inhabitants present. When I beheld these miserable creatures—men and women—the victims of drunkenness and other vices, with scarcely a rag to cover them—some with only a scanty cloth wrapped round the middle of the body—I was more inclined to believe myself in the interior of Africa than in the immediate vicinity of the capital city of the English possessions in that part of India.

Kossely, a village which contains only a few houses, though there is a bungalow there, is about a mile distant from the arm of the sea that separates Salsette from the continent. An excellent ferry, supported by the government, enabled me to cross over with my luggage to the little village of Kosla. Here I was obliged to have recourse to the judge as a protection against the chicanery of my camel-drivers. Though it was Sunday, my application was listened to, and justice done.

The camel-drivers had been hired in Maw, and engaged to go on to Bombay, and this agreement had been ratified by the police. But after crossing the ferry, as I mentioned, they refused to proceed to Bombay, which was still two days' march distant. It was for this reason that I was obliged to appeal to the judge. I wanted to find some other means of transporting my luggage, and I wished to guard against the possibility of my conduct being misrepresented at Maw. Notwithstanding the unseasonable time at which I appeared before the magistrate, I received every attention, and all the help that I sought. The camel-drivers had disappeared, and I deposited the money that was due to them in the hands of the judge. A short time afterwards, I received a letter from him, enclosing the deposited sum, as he had not heard anything more about the persons to whom it was due. This sum, which to a camel-driver could not be a trifle, I forwarded to Maw.

This little incident, which is nothing extraordinary in India, will serve to give an idea of the mode of proceeding there. Two months' wages ought to have been of importance to people whose sole means of support was what they earned by their camels, and yet they ran the risk of losing this rather than perform the two days' march that would have brought them to Bombay. The excuse they alleged was, that they could not get fodder for the camels in Bombay; but this could not be literally true, for, if not in the city, they could have found abundant provision for their cattle in the vicinity. The real motive of their refusal I believe to be the apprehension that, if they entered Bombay, their camels would be seized by the government authorities, and compelled to work in their service. Though for this work they would receive the ordinary rate of wages, the idea of compulsion was intolerable. Besides, their stay in Bombay might be prolonged to a very disagreeable length. They even ran the risk of being sent elsewhere at the will of their self-constituted employers, if they once fell into their hands.

Whatever may have been the motives of their conduct, the camel-drivers ran away, and left the payment of their wages dependent on the conscientiousness of a man with whom they had broken their engagement. If I had been satisfied that I had done enough when the judge returned the money, or if, *par hazard*, I had not known the names of these men, they might never have received their wages. This, however, tends very much to the honour of English gentlemen in India. They are the only Europeans with whom the natives come in contact, and this confidence in their honesty is a respectable tribute to the English character.

The road to Gurla leads through a part of the island that is a perfect jungle, and the only evidences of cultivation are to be found in the mangoe trees. There are no fields to be seen, except the small badly-kept strips of land that surround the drinking-houses.

That we become quickly accustomed to things which but a short time before seemed very strange, and that we are as easily weaned from them, is well known. My long absence from Europe, and desuetude of European customs, were perhaps the cause of my indignation when I beheld these drinking-houses—these stalls of bestiality. I felt an inclination to spit in the faces of the "inn-keepers," so despicable did their occupation seem to me. The trade is followed only by Portuguese and half-caste men. A Hindoo who has any trace of goodness will not practise it. These houses are generally found at a distance from the city; and the Europeans who keep them are, for the most part, men who have lost all chance of advancing their social position.

Drawing still closer to Bombay, the landscape assumes a more lively aspect. Villages and well-tilled fields are to be seen, but most conspicuous is the aamka deracht. The fruit of this beautiful tree, the mangoe of Bombay, is renowned throughout India for its size and flavour. The esteem in which the mangoes of the district are held is not a distinction acquired in modern times. When the Mogul emperors reigned in Delhi, the Bombay mangoes were to be seen every day on their table. These mangoes have not the flavour of turpentine, which is peculiar to those of Bengal.

During the last day's march, before reaching Bombay, we passed some country-houses belonging to native merchants. The appearance of these villas say distinctly that they are the offspring of better days, and that their possessors bestow now little care and attention on them. The aspect of the environs continues to improve until we reach Pareil, which is about six miles from Bombay.

Bombay is daily increasing in extent, which

must naturally happen in a city that is the focus of the commerce of an immense district and the seat of government. It has already extended far beyond the walls of the old town, and indeed a line of connection, kept up by houses, gardens and bazaars, prolongs the city even to Pareil.

That the city reached this point seemed to be the opinion of my servants, who pitched my tent in Pareil, though I had expressed my intention of taking up my abode in Bombay; but I was not sorry to be removed from the toil and tumult of a city. Now that I was on the point of entering again within the bounds of European civilization, I lingered still with melancholy pleasure within those wide domains where Nature reigns supreme, and where, untrammelled by human laws, roaming through dark forests, and over widely-extending plains, I had so long enjoyed unfettered freedom.

Two days after my arrival, I entered the city, and was busy arranging my goods and chattels in an English hotel, established in Bombay, when Captain d'Arcy was announced. He came on the part of Sir George Arthur, to invite me to remain with him at Pareil, during the time that I purposed to stay in India. All my objections were overruled, and I was obliged to yield. Bombay is celebrated for the hospitality of its inhabitants; and I can add my testimony in support of the general praise. I shall ever remember with pleasure the weeks I passed at Sir George Arthur's.

The site of the government-house at Pareil is very well selected. It is apart from all the confusion and bustle of the town, in a healthful and airy situation, surrounded by an open space, in which are grass-plats, flowers, and groups of trees. The apartments are spacious, and so arranged as, in this warm climate, to afford an agreeable coolness.

True refinement and elegance in social life exercise a beneficial effect on all. Even the rude spirit, fresh from the wilderness, becomes softened down under these benign influences, and is willing to forget the desert and the forest, and the wild beauties of untutored nature.

In consequence of the illness of Lady Arthur, the circle at government-house was not very large. It generally consisted of Sir George, Captain d'Arcy, A.D.C., Mr. Erskine, the governor's private secretary, and myself. Mr. Erskine's occupations did not allow me to enjoy much of his society, but Captain d'Arcy was always ready to join the many parties which were made to afford me an opportunity of seeing the curiosities of Bombay.

The rock temples of Elephanta, of which the wide-spread reputation had long since excited my curiosity, did not equal my expectations. They were neither so extensive nor so massive as they had been described to me. Their position is most happily chosen, for anybody not directly in front of the rock in which they are excavated, would never suspect that it contained in its bosom these celebrated works of art. The locality is in every way favourable, for the front layers of the rock present a solid mass, so that the workmen were not obliged to cut deep into the mountain before commencing their architectural operations. To add to the beauty of the situation, these lehnas are separated from the sea only by a handsome bowling-green, planted with trees and shrubs. The chief entrance is on that side of the temple that faces the sea.

Directly opposite to this entrance, and hewn in the solid rock, which forms the furthermost wall of the temple, is the well known three-headed colossal bust. The proportions of this figure are projected on so large a scale, that the hand measures six feet in length. To the left of this figure, in which many Christian priests have fancied that they beheld a representation of the Trinity, there is a figure of Bremma, as the word is pronounced, or Brahma as it is written. On the right hand Siva, or Schiva appears as Arinaria, or Ardhanaria.

Turning on the right, we found an inner temple, containing a Schiva-stone; stepping farther in the same direction, we stood beneath the blue sky. Turning to the other side of the temple, and walking through different rows of pillars, we stepped into the open air, through a way which must have been once the chief entrance to the temple, for opposite to this, through the pillared walks of the inner temple, lies the sanctum, which contains the

Schiva-stone. This stone was evidently the chief object of worship, and not the triple-headed figure, which, though three-faced, could not be called the Trimukhe, which is peculiar to the sacred shield of the Jayns.

That this lehna is a Schiva temple, admits of no doubt, and I will further remark that all the Indian temples are dedicated to Schiva or Mahadeo, and in later times fell into the hands of the followers of Vischnu. Therefore Schiva remains to this day in India, what his name signifies, the Mahadeo (chief god.)

Not far from the entrance towards the sea, there is a figure of Schiva, with the chain skulls. This is very well executed. In front of the chief entrance, at least that which I am disposed to consider as such, there is a small room, which must at one time have been a part of the temple. In this there is a well of beautiful clear water.

Having mentioned Elephanta I will say a few words, *en passant*, of Salsette. The chief temple is not very large, though handsomer than that at Elephanta. The architecture is strikingly like that of the lehnas at Nasak.

This resemblance is especially observable in the columns. The remaining rock-hewn structures are small, and strengthen me in the opinion that these excavations were originally intended for dwellings, and in this respect Salsette may, with better reason than Mahabalipura on the Coromandel coast, be considered a rock-hewn city, if we can consent to give the name of "city" to an extent of surface that would not contain more than the population of a village.

For myself, I must say, that in Salsette I was more delighted with the forest than with the rock-temples. This is a bold expression considering the reputation that the latter have won for Salsette, and I would be almost tempted to withdraw it, when I consider the satisfaction I felt in the chief temple. The ornaments on one of the columns here, convinced me that what I had before suspected was correct, that the symbolical stone in the older Buddha temples at Adjinta, represented an altar, or place of sacrifice.

The ornamental sculpture in Salsette to which I have alluded, represents two elephants. There are karras, or vases, which seem to have been filled with fruits and flowers, laid on the altar, and upon which offerings are heaped. At the foot of the altar are two figures, whose brows are encircled with snake-headed crowns, and who are offering karras filled with fruit and flowers to the elephants. In the little compartment, on the left hand of the great temple, are some figures in good preservation. There are others, evidently Buddha figures, which are unfinished. I have already remarked the similarity that exists between the columns in this temple and those of the lehnas at Nasak. There are some in the temple of Salsette which seem to be the work of a later period than the rest of the structure.

I must not close these pages without making mention of the Parsees of Bombay. They do not live in the city, and form within themselves a close confraternity. The time that I passed in the neighbourhood was too short to allow me to learn many particulars about them. I can only say that they are of a lighter complexion than the Hindoos, and most graceful in their movements. The women, especially, wrapped in their red shawls, present a very picturesque appearance; they are, besides, modest in their manners, and moral in their lives. The men are active, and intelligent, and good men of business; those of the poorer class are excellent servants. There are some functions which they cannot discharge, their religious code forbidding them to kindle fires or extinguish lights. To evade the difficulty that this prohibition entails, they sometimes wrap the flame of the candle in a cloth, and effect by this contrivance, what they dare not directly perform.

My friends in Pareil allowed no opportunity to pass that could procure me amusement. In company with Captain d'Arcy and Mr. Erskine, I went to a soirée at the house of a rich Parsee. The evening passed most agreeably. The company consisted of English, as well as native ladies and gentlemen. The Parsee portion of the society excited my particular admiration. They exhibited all the ease and elegance of manner that one finds in the highest European circles, and the ladies were most attractive with their slender forms and delicately-moulded features. I cannot forbear mentioning the daughter of the house, who, if not beautiful, was extremely fascinating.

As far as personal beauty is concerned, a comparison between the English and native ladies must always be to the disadvantage of the latter; the beauty of the English being universally acknowledged, and their loveliness assumes a new and more interesting character in India. Their seclusion from sun and light in this warm climate, gives to their complexions a delicacy and transparency that lend to their whole appearance something so etherial and refined as to place them beyond all rivalry. The English ladies whom I met at Calcutta were the most beautiful that I saw in India. I thought they looked more lovely during the rainy season, when their health must have been most delicate.

To Europeans, the fair complexion will always appear the most beautiful. The nations that are black, brown or yellow, will naturally admire persons of their own hue. It is said that when the natives of Africa wish to portray the devil; they paint him white. This I think very possible; their opinion of white-complexioned men cannot be very good; and the blacks who, through illness, become pale, or whitish, present a hideous appearance.

I have said that fair-complexioned beauties appear to us the most lovely, and in this respect the British ladies possess a vast superiority over all others. But neither are the Indian ladies devoid of charms. In them we find, in the highest degree, delicacy of form, beauty of feature, and perfect symmetry. Central Asia, the Caucasus, and Asia Minor, hide within their romantic forests, their wild and lovely valleys, many a beauteous being, who, however, does not bloom unprized, for real beauty never fails to win adorers.

In Bombay, I consider myself, so to say, on European ground. As so many who have travelled in India have described this place, anything that I could say would be mere repetition. But though I do not intend to give a detailed account of the city, the remembrance of the days I passed there, and in Pareil, will be long engraven in my memory, and entwined with these feelings will be the profound esteem I conceived for the character of Sir George Arthur, as well as the warmest recollection of his kind and friendly conduct towards me.

My object in publishing an account of my travels was, to give to Europeans, unacquainted with the countries through which I passed, a picture of the character and customs of the natives of these foreign lands. A long residence in India, and an intercourse with the various classes of society there, gave me opportunities of studying the national character.

That men and women are essentially the same in every region of the globe is undeniably true. The same passions and the same propensities lurk in the bosom of the inhabitant of India and of Europe, modified by a difference in social circumstances, and the contrast existing, on many points, in the moral code of the various nations. Viewing the matter in this light, it must be admitted that the European often judges his Asiatic brother with undue severity. We should remember that theirs is a different civilization from ours, a different morality, and, above all, that they are under a different system of religious teaching. Is there not injustice, as well as bigotry, in applying to their actions the same test by which our own should be tried?

I have set down the incidents of my journey precisely as they occurred. Should they afford instruction or amusement to my readers, my object will be attained to a certain degree, but should the perusal of these pages arouse in his mind the spirit of inquiry, or awaken in his heart the gentler feelings of toleration and indulgence towards his fellow men, my fondest wish will have been fulfilled.

THE END.

LONDON:
Printed by Schulze and Co., 13, Poland Street.

MILITARY LIFE IN ALGERIA.

BY THE COUNT P. DE CASTELLANE.

2 vols. post 8vo. 21s.

TRAVELS IN INDIA AND KASHMIR.

BY BARON SCHONBERG.

2 vols. post 8vo. 21s.

WISE SAWS AND MODERN INSTANCES.

BY THE AUTHOR OF "SAM SLICK."

3 vols. post 8vo. 31s. 6d.

FAMILY ROMANCE;

OR, EPISODES IN

THE DOMESTIC ANNALS OF THE ARISTOCRACY.

BY J. B. BURKE, ESQ.

Author of "The Peerage," "Anecdotes of the Aristocracy," &c.

2 vols. post 8vo. 21s.

MEMOIRS OF JOHN ABERNETHY, F.R.S.,

WITH A VIEW OF

HIS WRITINGS, LECTURES, AND CHARACTER.

BY GEORGE MACILWAIN, F.R.C.S.,

Author of "Medicine and Surgery One Inductive Science," &c.

2 vols. post 8vo. 21s.

NARRATIVE OF A FIVE YEARS'

JOURNEY ROUND THE WORLD,

FROM 1847 TO 1852.

BY F. GERSTAUKER.

3 vols. post 8vo.

A NEW WORK.

BY THE AUTHOR OF

"EMILIA WYNDHAM."

In 1 volume.

AUTOBIOGRAPHY OF

AN ENGLISH SOLDIER

IN THE UNITED STATES' ARMY.

2 vols. post 8vo. 21s.

The Following Are Lately Published.

LORD GEORGE BENTINCK:

A POLITICAL BIOGRAPHY.

BY THE RIGHT HON. B. DISRAELI, M.P.

FIFTH AND CHEAPER EDITION, REVISED. Post 8vo. 10s. 6d.

MEMOIRS OF THE

BARONESS D'OBERKIRCH,

ILLUSTRATIVE OF THE SECRET HISTORY OF

THE COURTS OF FRANCE, RUSSIA, AND GERMANY.

WRITTEN BY HERSELF,

And Edited by Her Grandson, the COUNT DE MONTBRISON.

3 Vols. Post 8vo., 31s. 6d.

THE LIFE OF MARIE DE MEDICIS,

QUEEN OF FRANCE,

CONSORT OF HENRY IV., AND REGENT UNDER LOUIS XIII.

BY MISS PARDOE,

Author of "Louis XIV. and the Court of France in the 17th Century," &c.

SECOND EDITION. 3 large vols. 8vo., with Fine Portraits, 42s.

ADVENTURES OF

THE CONNAUGHT RANGERS.

Second Series.

BY WILLIAM GRATTAN, ESQ.,

LATE LIEUTENANT CONNAUGHT RANGERS.

2 vols. post 8vo. 21s.

The Following Are Lately Published.

AUSTRALIA AS IT IS:

ITS SETTLEMENTS, FARMS, AND GOLD FIELDS.

BY F. LANCELOTT, ESQ.,

MINERALOGICAL SURVEYOR IN THE AUSTRALIAN COLONIES.

2 vols. post 8vo., 21s.

THE MARVELS OF SCIENCE,

AND THEIR TESTIMONY TO HOLY WRIT;

A POPULAR MANUAL OF THE SCIENCES.

BY S. W. FULLOM, ESQ.,

DEDICATED BY PERMISSION TO THE KING OF HANOVER.

THIRD EDITION, REVISED. Post 8vo. 10s. 6d.

REVELATIONS OF SIBERIA.

BY A BANISHED LADY.

SECOND EDITION. 2 vols. post 8vo., 21s.

THE LITERATURE AND ROMANCE

OF NORTHERN EUROPE:

A COMPLETE HISTORY OF THE LITERATURE OF SWEDEN, DENMARK, NORWAY, AND ICELAND, WITH COPIOUS SPECIMENS.

BY WILLIAM AND MARY HOWITT.

2 vols. post 8vo. 21s.

New Works of Fiction

By Distinguished Writers.

THE LIEUTENANT'S STORY.

BY LADY CATHARINE LONG,

AUTHOR OF "SIR ROLAND ASHTON," &c.

3 vols. (*Now Ready.*)

THE DEAN'S DAUGHTER.

BY MRS. GORE.

3 vols.

HARRY MUIR;

A STORY OF SCOTTISH LIFE.

BY THE AUTHOR OF "MARGARET MAITLAND," "ADAM GRAEME," &c.

3 vols.

A NEW NOVEL.

BY MRS. TROLLOPE.

3 vols.

New Works of Fiction

By Distinguished Writers.

THE JEALOUS WIFE.

BY MISS PARDOE.

3 vols.

CASTLE AVON.

BY THE AUTHOR OF

"EMILIA WYNDHAM," &c.

3 vols. (*Now Ready.*)

THE LONGWOODS

OF THE GRANGE.

BY THE AUTHOR OF "ADELAIDE LINDSAY."

3 vols.

BROOMHILL;

OR, THE COUNTY BEAUTIES.

3 vols. (*Now Ready.*)

as the general history of her times, and its effects on her character, and we have done so with singleness of heart, unbiassed by selfish interests or narrow views. Such as they were in life we have endeavoured to portray them, both in good and ill, without regard to any other considerations than the development of the *facts*. Their sayings, their doings, their manners, their costume, will be found faithfully chronicled in this work, which also includes the most interesting of their letters. The hope that the 'Lives of the Queens of England' might be regarded as a national work, honourable to the female character, and generally useful to society, has encouraged us to the completion of the task."

OPINIONS OF THE PRESS.

"These volumes have the fascination of romance united to the integrity of history. The work is written by a lady of considerable learning, indefatigable industry, and careful judgment. All these qualifications for a biographer and an historian she has brought to bear upon the subject of her volumes, and from them has resulted a narrative interesting to all, and more particularly interesting to that portion of the community to whom the more refined researches of literature afford pleasure and instruction. The whole work should be read, and no doubt will be read, by all who are anxious for information. It is a lucid arrangement of facts, derived from authentic sources, exhibiting a combination of industry, learning, judgment, and impartiality, not often met with in biographers of crowned heads."—*Times*.

"A remarkable and truly great historical work. In this series of biographies, in which the severe truth of history takes almost the wildness of romance, it is the singular merit of Miss Strickland that her research has enabled her to throw new light on many doubtful passages, to bring forth fresh facts, and to render every portion of our annals which she has described an interesting and valuable study. She has given a most valuable contribution to the history of England, and we have no hesitation in affirming that no one can be said to possess an accurate knowledge of the history of the country who has not studied this truly national work, which, in this new edition, has received all the aids that further research on the part of the author, and of embellishment on the part of the publishers, could tend to make it still more valuable, and still more attractive, than it had been in its original form."—*Morning Herald*.

"A most valuable and entertaining work. There is certainly no lady of our day who has devoted her pen to so beneficial a purpose as Miss Strickland. Nor is there any other whose works possess a deeper or more enduring interest. Miss Strickland is to our mind the first literary lady of the age."—*Morning Chronicle*.

"We must pronounce Miss Strickland beyond all comparison the most entertaining historian in the English language. She is certainly a woman of powerful and active mind, as well as of scrupulous justice and honesty of purpose."—*Morning Post*.

"Miss Strickland has made a very judicious use of many authentic MS. authorities not previously collected, and the result is a most interesting addition to our biographical library."—*Quarterly Review*.

"A valuable contribution to historical knowledge. It contains a mass of every kind of historical matter of interest, which industry and research could collect. We have derived much entertainment and instruction from the work."—*Athenæum*.

BURKE'S PEERAGE AND BARONETAGE,

FOR 1853.—IN THE PRESS.

NEW EDITION, REVISED AND CORRECTED THROUGHOUT FROM THE PERSONAL COMMUNICATIONS OF THE NOBILITY, &c.

With the ARMS (1500 in number) accurately engraved, and incorporated with the Text. In 1 vol. (comprising as much matter as twenty ordinary volumes), 38s. bound.

The following is a List of the Principal Contents of this Standard Work:—

I. A full and interesting history of each order of the English Nobility, showing its origin, rise, titles, immunities, privileges, &c.

II. A complete Memoir of the Queen and Royal Family, forming a brief genealogical History of the Sovereign of this country, and deducing the descent of the Plantagenets, Tudors, Stuarts, and Guelphs, through their various ramifications. To this section is appended a list of those Peers who inherit the distinguished honour of Quartering the Royal Arms of Plantagenet.

III. An Authentic Table of Precedence.

IV. A perfect History of All the Peers and Baronets, with the fullest details of their ancestors and descendants, and particulars respecting every collateral member of each family, and all intermarriages, &c.

V. The Spiritual Lords.

VI. Foreign Noblemen, subjects by birth of the British Crown.

VII. Peerages claimed.

VIII. Surnames of Peers and Peeresses, with Heirs Apparent and Presumptive.

IX. Courtesy titles of Eldest Sons.

X. Peerages of the Three Kingdoms in order of Precedence.

XI. Baronets in order of Precedence.

XII. Privy Councillors of England and Ireland.

XIII. Daughters of Peers married to Commoners.

XIV. All the Orders of Knighthood, with every Knight and all the Knights Bachelors.

XV. Mottoes translated, with poetical illustrations.

"The most complete, the most convenient, and the cheapest work of the kind ever given to the public."—*Sun.*

"The best genealogical and heraldic dictionary of the Peerage and Baronetage, and the first authority on all questions affecting the aristocracy."—*Globe.*

"For the amazing quantity of personal and family history, admirable arrangement of details, and accuracy of information, this genealogical and heraldic dictionary is without a rival. It is now the standard and acknowledged book of reference upon all questions touching pedigree, and direct or collateral affinity with the titled aristocracy. The lineage of each distinguished house is deduced through all the various ramifications. Every collateral branch, however remotely connected, is introduced; and the alliances are so carefully inserted, as to show, in all instances, the connexion which so intimately exists between the titled and untitled aristocracy. We have also much most entertaining historical matter, and many very curious and interesting family traditions. The work is, in fact, a complete cyclopædia of the whole titled classes of the empire, supplying all the information that can possibly be desired on the subject."—*Morning Post.*

"The 'Peerage' and the 'Landed Gentry' of Mr. Burke are two works of public utility—constantly referred to by all classes of society, and rarely opened without being found to supply the information sought. They are accessions of value to our books of reference, and few who write or talk much about English Peers and English Landed Gentry, can well be looked on as safe authorities without a knowledge of the contents of Mr. Burke's careful compilations."—*Athenæum.*

BURKE'S HISTORY OF THE LANDED GENTRY

A Genealogical Dictionary

OF THE WHOLE OF THE UNTITLED ARISTOCRACY OF ENGLAND, SCOTLAND, AND IRELAND:

Comprising Particulars of 100,000 Individuals connected with them.

In 2 volumes, royal 8vo, including the Supplement, beautifully printed in double columns, comprising more matter than 30 ordinary volumes, price only 2*l.* 2s., elegantly bound,

WITH A SEPARATE INDEX, GRATIS.

CONTAINING REFERENCES TO THE NAMES OF EVERY PERSON MENTIONED.

The Landed Gentry of England are so closely connected with the stirring records of its eventful history, that some acquaintance with them is a matter of necessity with the legislator, the lawyer, the historical student, the speculator in politics, and the curious in topographical and antiquarian lore; and even the very spirit of ordinary curiosity will prompt to a desire to trace the origin and progress of those families whose influence pervades the towns and villages of our land. This work furnishes such a mass of authentic information in regard to all the principal families in the kingdom as has never before been attempted to be brought together. It relates to the untitled families of rank, as the "Peerage and Baronetage" does to the titled, and forms, in fact, a peerage of the untitled aristocracy. It embraces the whole of the landed interest, and is indispensable to the library of every gentleman. The great cost attending the production of this National Work, the first of its kind, induces the publisher to hope that the heads of all families recorded in its pages will supply themselves with copies.

"A work of this kind is of a national value. Its utility is not merely temporary, but it will exist and be acknowledged as long as the families whose names and genealogies are recorded in it continue to form an integral portion of the English constitution As a correct record of descent, no family should be without it. The untitled aristocracy have in this great work as perfect a dictionary of their genealogical history, family connexions, and heraldic rights, as the peerage and baronetage. It will be an enduring and trustworthy record."—*Morning Post.*

"A work in which every gentleman will find a domestic interest, as it contains the fullest account of every known family in the United Kingdom. It is a dictionary of all names, families, and their origin,—of every man's neighbour and friend, if not of his own relatives and immediate connexions. It cannot fail to be of the greatest utility to professional men in their researches respecting the members of different families, heirs to property, &c. Indeed, it will become as necessary as a Directory in every office."—*Bell's Messenger.*

DIARY AND CORRESPONDENCE

OF

JOHN EVELYN, F.R.S.,

Author of "Sylva," &c.

A NEW EDITION, REVISED AND ENLARGED, WITH NUMEROUS ADDITIONAL LETTERS NOW FIRST PUBLISHED.

UNIFORM WITH THE NEW EDITION OF PEPYS' DIARY.

In 4 vols., post 8vo, price 10s. 6d. each.

N.B.—Vols. III. and IV., containing "The Correspondence," may be had separately, to complete sets.

The Diary and Correspondence of John Evelyn has long been regarded as an invaluable record of opinions and events, as well as the most interesting exposition we possess of the manners, taste, learning, and religion of this country, during the latter half of the seventeenth century. The Diary comprises observations on the politics, literature, and science of his age, during his travels in France and Italy; his residence in England towards the latter part of the Protectorate, and his connexion with the Courts of Charles II and the two subsequent reigns, interspersed with a vast number of original anecdotes of the most celebrated persons of that period. To the Diary is subjoined the Correspondence of Evelyn with many of his distinguished contemporaries; also Original Letters from Sir Edward Nicholas, private secretary to King Charles I., during some important periods of that reign, with the King's answers; and numerous letters from Sir Edward Hyde (Lord Clarendon) to Sir Edward Nicholas, and to Sir Richard Brown, Ambassador to France, during the exile of the British Court.

A New Edition of this interesting work having been long demanded, the greatest pains have been taken to render it as complete as possible, by a careful re-examination of the original Manuscript, and by illustrating it with such annotations as will make the reader more conversant with the numerous subjects referred to by the Diarist.

"It has been justly observed that as long as Virtue and Science hold their abode in this island, the memory of Evelyn will be held in the utmost veneration. Indeed, no change of fashion, no alteration of taste, no revolution of science, have impaired, or can impair, his celebrity. The youth who looks forward to an inheritance which he is under no temptation to increase, will do well to bear the example of Evelyn in his mind, as containing nothing but what is imitable, and nothing but what is good. All persons, indeed, may find in his character something for imitation, but for an English gentleman he is the perfect model."—*Quarterly Review.*

LIVES OF THE PRINCESSES OF ENGLAND.

By MRS EVERETT GREEN,

EDITOR OF THE "LETTERS OF ROYAL AND ILLUSTRIOUS LADIES."

4 vols., post 8vo, with Illustrations, 10s. 6d. each, bound.

OPINIONS OF THE PRESS.

"A most agreeable book. The authoress, already favourably known to the learned world by her excellent collection of 'Letters of Royal and Illustrious Ladies," has executed her task with great skill and fidelity. Every page displays careful research and accuracy. There is a graceful combination of sound, historical erudition, with an air of romance and adventure that is highly pleasing, and renders the work at once an agreeable companion of the boudoir, and a valuable addition to the historical library. Mrs. Green has entered upon an untrodden path, and gives to her biographies an air of freshness and novelty very alluring. The first two volumes (including the Lives of twenty-five Princesses) carry us from the daughters of the Conqueror to the family of Edward I.—a highly interesting period, replete with curious illustrations of the genius and manners of the Middle Ages. Such works, from the truthfulness of their spirit, furnish a more lively picture of the times than even the graphic, though delusive, pencil of Scott and James."—*Britannia.*

"The vast utility of the task undertaken by the gifted author of this interesting book can only be equalled by the skill, ingenuity, and research displayed in its accomplishment. The field Mrs. Green has selected is an untrodden one. Mrs. Green, on giving to the world a work which will enable us to arrive at a correct idea of the private histories and personal characters of the royal ladies of England, has done sufficient to entitle her to the respect and gratitude of the country. The labour of her task was exceedingly great, involving researches, not only into English records and chronicles, but into those of almost every civilised country in Europe. The style of Mrs. Green is admirable. She has a fine perception of character and manners, a penetrating spirit of observation, and singular exactness of judgment. The memoirs are richly fraught with the spirit of romantic adventure."—*Morning Post.*

"This work is a worthy companion to Miss Strickland's admirable 'Queens of England.' In one respect the subject-matter of these volumes is more interesting, because it is more diversified than that of the 'Queens of England.' That celebrated work, although its heroines were, for the most part, foreign Princesses, related almost entirely to the history of this country. The Princesses of England, on the contrary, are themselves English, but their lives are nearly all connected with foreign nations. Their biographies, consequently, afford us a glimpse of the manners and customs of the chief European kingdoms, a circumstance which not only gives to the work the charm of variety, but which is likely to render it peculiarly useful to the general reader, as it links together by association the contemporaneous history of various nations. The histories are related with an earnest simplicity and copious explicitness. The reader is informed without being wearied, and alternately enlivened by some spirited description, or touched by some pathetic or tender episode. We cordially commend Mrs. Everett Green's production to general attention; it is (necessarily) as useful as history, and fully as entertaining as romance."—*Sun.*

THE LIFE AND REIGN OF CHARLES I.

By I. DISRAELI.

A NEW EDITION. REVISED BY THE AUTHOR, AND EDITED BY HIS SON, THE RT. HON. B. DISRAELI, M.P.

2 vols., 8vo, uniform with the "Curiosities of Literature," 28s. bound.

"By far the most important work on the important age of Charles I. that modern times have produced."—*Quarterly Review.*

MEMOIRS OF HORACE WALPOLE

AND HIS CONTEMPORARIES,

INCLUDING NUMEROUS ORIGINAL LETTERS, FROM STRAWBERRY HILL.

EDITED BY

ELIOT WARBURTON.

2 vols. 8vo, with Portraits, 16s. bound.

Perhaps no name of modern times is productive of so many pleasant associations as that of "Horace Walpole," and certainly no name was ever more intimately connected with so many different subjects of importance in connexion with Literature, Art, Fashion, and Politics. The position of various members of his family connecting Horace Walpole with the Cabinet, the Court, and the Legislature—his own intercourse with those characters who became remarkable for brilliant social and intellectual qualities—and his reputation as a Wit, a Scholar, and a Virtuoso, cannot fail to render his Memoirs equally amusing and instructive. They nearly complete the chain of mixed personal, political, and literary history, commencing with "Evelyn" and "Pepys," carried forward by "Swift's Journal and Correspondence," and ending almost in our own day with the histories of Mr. Macaulay and Lord Mahon.

"These Memoirs form a necessary addition to the library of every English gentleman. Besides its historical value, which is very considerable, the work cannot be estimated too highly as a book of mere amusement."—*Standard.*

MADAME PULSZKY'S MEMOIRS.

Comprising Full and Interesting Details of

THE LATE EVENTS IN HUNGARY.

With an Historical Introduction by FRANCIS PULSZKY, late Under-Secretary of State to Ferdinand, Emperor of Austria and King of Hungary. 2 vols., post 8vo, 21s. bound.

THE DIARIES AND CORRESPONDENCE OF THE

EARLS OF CLARENDON AND ROCHESTER;

Comprising important Particulars of the Revolution, &c.

Published from the Original MSS. With Notes. 2 vols., with fine Portraits and Plates, bound, 1*l.* 11s. 6d.

BURKE'S DICTIONARY OF THE EXTINCT, DORMANT, & ABEYANT PEERAGES

OF ENGLAND, SCOTLAND, AND IRELAND.

Beautifully printed, in 1 vol. 8vo, containing 800 double-column pages, 21s. bound.

This work, formed on a plan precisely similar to that of Mr. Burke's popular Dictionary of the present Peerage and Baronetage, comprises those peerages which have been suspended or extinguished since the Conquest, particularising the members of each family in each generation, and bringing the lineage, in all possible cases, through either collaterals or females, down to existing houses. It connects, in many instances, the new with the old nobility, and it will in all cases show the cause which has influenced the revival of an extinct dignity in a new creation. It should be particularly noticed, that this new work appertains nearly as much to extant as to extinct persons of distinction; for though dignities pass away, it rarely occurs that whole families do.'

CONTENTS.

1. Peerages of England extinct by failure of issue, attainder, &c., alphabetically, according to Surnames.
2. Baronies by Writ—England—in abeyance, and still vested probably in existing heirs.
3. Extinct and Abeyant Peerages of England, according to titles.
4. Charters of Freedom—Magna Charta—Charter of Forests.
5. Roll of Battel Abbey.
6. Peerages of Ireland, extinct by failure of issue, attainder, &c., alphabetically, according to Surnames.
7. Baronies by Writ—Ireland—in abeyance.
8. Peerages of Ireland, extinct and abeyant, alphabetically, according to Titles.
9. Peerages of Scotland, extinct by failure of issue, attainder, &c., alphabetically, according to Surnames.
10. Extinct Peerages of Scotland, alphabetically, according to Titles.

MEMOIRS OF SCIPIO DE RICCI,

LATE BISHOP OF PISTOIA AND PRATO;

REFORMER OF CATHOLICISM IN TUSCANY.

Cheaper Edition, 2 vols. 8vo, 12s. bound.

The leading feature of this important work is its application to the great question now at issue between our Protestant and Catholic fellow-subjects. It contains a complete *exposé* of the Romish Church Establishment during the eighteenth century, and of the abuses of the Jesuits throughout the greater part of Europe. Many particulars of the most thrilling kind are brought to light.

MADAME CAMPAN'S MEMOIRS

OF THE COURT OF MARIE ANTOINETTE.

Cheaper Edition, 2 vols. 8vo, with Portraits, price only 12s.—The same in French, 7s.

"We have seldom perused so entertaining a work. It is as a mirror of the most splendid Court in Europe, at a time when the monarchy had not been shorn of any of its beams, that it is particularly worthy of attention."—*Chronicle.*

LIFE AND CORRESPONDENCE OF JOHN LOCKE.

By LORD KING. 2 vols. 16s.

HISTORIC SCENES.

By AGNES STRICKLAND.

Author of "Lives of the Queens of England," &c. 1 vol., post 8vo, elegantly bound, with Portrait of the Author, 10s. 6d.

"This attractive volume is replete with interest. Like Miss Strickland's former works, it will be found, we doubt not, in the hands of youthful branches of a family, as well as in those of their parents, to all and each of whom it cannot fail to be alike amusing and instructive."—*Britannia.*

LETTERS OF ROYAL AND ILLUSTRIOUS LADIES OF GREAT BRITAIN.

Now first published from the Originals, with Historical Notices.

By MRS. EVERETT GREEN,

Author of "Lives of the Princesses of England."

Cheaper Edition. 3 vols., with Facsimile Autographs, &c., 15s. bound.

GENÈRAL PEPE'S NARRATIVE OF THE WAR IN ITALY,

FROM 1847 to 1850; INCLUDING THE SIEGE OF VENICE.

Now first published from the original Italian Manuscript.
Cheaper Edition, 2 vols., post 8vo, 12s. bound.

"We predict that posterity will accept General Pepe as the historian of the great Italian movement of the nineteenth century. His work is worthy of all commendation."—*Standard.*

THE

REV. R. MILMAN'S LIFE OF TASSO.

Cheaper Edition in 2 vols., post 8vo, 12s. bound.

"Mr. Milman's book has considerable merit. He has evidently, in his interesting biography of Tasso, undertaken a labour of love. His diligence has been great, his materials are copious and well-arranged, and his sketches of the poet's contemporaries form agreeable episodes in the narrative of Tasso's works and woes."—*Edinburgh Review.*

MEMOIRS AND CORRESPONDENCE OF

SIR ROBERT MURRAY KEITH, K.B.,

Minister Plenipotentiary at the Courts of Dresden, Copenhagen, and Vienna, from 1769 to 1793; with Biographical Memoirs of

QUEEN CAROLINE MATILDA, SISTER OF GEORGE III.

2 vols., post 8vo, with Portraits, 21s. bound.

"A large portion of this important and highly interesting work consists of letters, that we venture to say will bear a comparison for sterling wit, lively humour, entertaining gossip, piquant personal anecdotes, and brilliant pictures of social life, in its highest phases, both at home and abroad, with those of Horace Walpole himself."—*Court Journal.*

CAPTAIN CRAWFORD'S REMINISCENCES

OF ADMIRALS SIR E. OWEN, SIR B. HALLOWELL CAREW, AND OTHER DISTINGUISHED COMMANDERS.

2 vols., post 8vo, with Portraits, 12s. bound.

"A work which cannot fail of being popular in every portion of our sea-girt isle, and of being read with delight by all who feel interested in the right hand of our country—its Navy."—*Plymouth Herald.*

REVELATIONS OF PRINCE TALLEYRAND.

By M. COLMACHE,

THE PRINCE'S PRIVATE SECRETARY.

Second Edition, 1 volume, post 8vo, with Portrait, 10s. 6d. bound.

"We have perused this work with extreme interest. It is a portrait of Talleyrand drawn by his own hand."—*Morning Post.*

"A more interesting work has not issued from the press for many years. It is in truth a complete Boswell sketch of the greatest diplomatist of the age."—*Sunday Times.*

HISTORY OF THE WAR IN GERMANY AND FRANCE IN 1813 & 1814.

By Lieut.-Gen. the MARQUIS OF LONDONDERRY, G.C.B., &c. &c., 21s.

Now ready, VOLUME XI., price 5s., of

M. A. THIERS' HISTORY OF FRANCE,

FROM THE PERIOD OF THE CONSULATE IN 1800, TO THE BATTLE OF WATERLOO.

A SEQUEL TO HIS HISTORY OF THE FRENCH REVOLUTION.

Having filled at different times the high offices of Minister of the Interior, of Finance, of Foreign Affairs, and President of the Council, M. Thiers has enjoyed facilities beyond the reach of every other biographer of Napoleon for procuring, from exclusive and authentic sources, the choicest materials for his present work. As guardian to the archives of the state, he had access to diplomatic papers and other documents of the highest importance, hitherto known only to a privileged few, and the publication of which cannot fail to produce a great sensation. From private sources, M. Thiers, it appears, has also derived much valuable information. Many interesting memoirs, diaries, and letters, all hitherto unpublished, and most of them destined for political reasons to remain so, have been placed at his disposal; while all the leading characters of the empire, who were alive when the author undertook the present history, have supplied him with a mass of incidents and anecdotes which have never before appeared in print, and the accuracy and value of which may be inferred from the fact of these parties having been themselves eye-witnesses of, or actors in, the great events of the period.

*** To prevent disappointment, the public are requested to be particular in giving their orders for "COLBURN'S AUTHORISED TRANSLATION."

HISTORY OF THE HOUSE OF COMMONS;

FROM THE CONVENTION PARLIAMENT OF 1688-9, TO THE PASSING OF THE REFORM BILL IN 1832.

By WM. CHARLES TOWNSEND, ESQ., M.A. 2 vols. 8vo, 12s. bound.

"We have here a collection of biographical notices of all the Speakers who have presided during the hundred and forty-four years above defined, and of several Members of Parliament the most distinguished in that period. Much useful and curious information is scattered throughout the volumes."—*Quarterly Review.*

DIARY AND MEMOIRS OF SOPHIA DOROTHEA,

CONSORT OF GEORGE I.

Now first published from the Originals.
Cheaper Edition, 2 vols., 8vo, with Portrait, 12s. bound.

"A book of marvellous revelations, establishing beyond all doubt the perfect innocence of the beautiful, highly-gifted, and inhumanly-treated Sophia Dorothea."—*Naval and Military Gazette.*

LETTERS OF MARY QUEEN OF SCOTS.

Illustrative of Her Personal History.
Edited, with an Historical Introduction and Notes,
By AGNES STRICKLAND.

Cheaper Edition, with numerous Additions, uniform with Miss Strickland's "Lives of the Queens of England." 2 vols., post 8vo, with Portrait, &c., 12s. bound.

"The best collection of authentic memorials relative to the Queen of Scots that has ever appeared."—*Morning Chronicle.*

MEMOIRS OF MADEMOISELLE DE MONTPENSIER.

Written by HERSELF. 3 vols., post 8vo, with Portrait.

"One of the most delightful and deeply-interesting works we have read for a long time."—*Weekly Chronicle.*

LADY BLESSINGTON'S JOURNAL

OF

HER CONVERSATIONS WITH LORD BYRON.

Cheaper Edition, in 8vo, embellished with
Portraits of Lady Blessington and Lord Byron, price only 7s. bound.

"The best thing that has been written on Lord Byron."—*Spectator.*
"Universally acknowledged to be delightful."—*Athenæum.*

ADVENTURES OF A SOLDIER,

Being the Memoirs of EDWARD COSTELLO, of the Rifle Brigade, late Captain in the British Legion;

Comprising Narratives of the Campaigns in the Peninsula under the Duke of Wellington, and the Civil War in Spain.

New and Cheaper Edition, with Portrait of the Author, 3s. 6d. bound.

ANECDOTES OF THE ARISTOCRACY,

AND

EPISODES IN ANCESTRAL STORY.

By J. BERNARD BURKE, Esq.,

Author of "The History of the Landed Gentry," "The Peerage and Baronetage," &c.

SECOND AND CHEAPER EDITION, 2 vols., post 8vo, 21s. bound.

"Mr. Burke has here given us the most curious incidents, the most stirring tales, and the most remarkable circumstances connected with the histories, public and private, of our noble houses and aristocratic families, and has put them into a shape which will preserve them in the library, and render them the favourite study of those who are interested in the romance of real life. These stories, with all the reality of established fact, read with as much spirit as the tales of Boccacio, and are as full of strange matter for reflection and amazement."—*Britannia.*

"We cannot estimate too highly the interest of Mr. Burke's entertaining and instructive work. For the curious nature of the details, the extraordinary anecdotes related, the strange scenes described, it would be difficult to find a parallel for it. It will be read by every one."—*Sunday Times.*

ROMANTIC RECORDS OF DISTINGUISHED FAMILIES.

BEING THE SECOND SERIES OF "ANECDOTES OF THE ARISTOCRACY."

By J. B. BURKE, Esq.

2 vols., post 8vo, 21s. bound.

"From the copious materials afforded by the history of the English Aristocracy, Mr. Burke has made another and a most happy selection, adding a second wing to his interesting picture-gallery. Some of the most striking incidents on record in the annals of high and noble families are here presented to view."—*John Bull.*

MR. DISRAELI'S CONINGSBY.

CHEAP STANDARD EDITION, WITH A NEW PREFACE.
In 1 vol., with Portrait, 6s. bound.

"We are glad to see that the finest work of Disraeli has been sent out in the same shape as those of Dickens, Bulwer, and other of our best novelists, at such a price as to place them within the reach of the most moderate means. 'Coningsby' has passed from the popularity of a season to an enduring reputation as a standard work. It is a valuable contribution to popular literature."—*Weekly Chronicle.*

WORKS OF LADY MORGAN.

1. WOMAN AND HER MASTER. A History of the Female Sex from the earliest Period. 2 vols., 12s.
2. THE BOOK OF THE BOUDOIR. 2 vols., 10s.
3. LIFE AND TIMES OF SALVATOR ROSA. 2 vols., 12s.
4. THE O'BRIENS AND THE O'FLAHERTYS. 4 vols., 14s.

GERMANY;
ITS COURTS AND PEOPLE.

BY THE AUTHOR OF "MILDRED VERNON."

Second and Cheaper Edition. 2 vols. 8vo, 21s. bound.

"An important, yet most amusing work, throwing much and richly-coloured light on matters with which every one desires to be informed. All the courts and people of Germany are passed in vivid review before us. The account of the Austrians, Magyars, and Croats, will be found especially interesting. In many of its lighter passages the work may bear a comparison with Lady Mary Wortley Montagu's Letters."—*Morning Chronicle.*

LORD LINDSAY'S LETTERS ON THE HOLY LAND.

FOURTH EDITION, Revised and Corrected, 1 vol., post 8vo, 6s. bound.

"Lord Lindsay has felt and recorded what he saw with the wisdom of a philosopher, and the faith of an enlightened Christian."—*Quarterly Review.*

THE SPIRIT OF THE EAST.

By D. URQUHART, Esq., M.P. 2 vols., 16s.

SIR HENRY WARD'S ACCOUNT OF MEXICO, THE MINING COMPANIES, &c.

2 vols., with Plates and Maps, 21s.

THE CRESCENT AND THE CROSS;

OR,

ROMANCE AND REALITIES OF EASTERN TRAVEL.

By ELIOT WARBURTON, Esq.

NINTH AND CHEAPER EDITION, 1 vol., with numerous Illustrations, 10s. 6d. bound.

HOCHELAGA;

OR,

ENGLAND IN THE NEW WORLD.

Edited by ELIOT WARBURTON, Esq.,

Author of "The Crescent and the Cross."

FOURTH AND CHEAPER EDITION, 2 vols., post 8vo, with Illustrations, 10s. 6d. bound.

"We recommend 'Hochelaga' most heartily, in case any of our readers may as yet be unacquainted with it."—*Quarterly Review.*

LIGHTS AND SHADES OF MILITARY LIFE.

Edited by Lieut.-Gen. Sir CHARLES NAPIER, G.C.B., Commander-in-Chief in India, &c. 1 vol., 8vo, 10s. 6d. bound.

"A narrative of stirring interest, which should be in the hands of every officer in her Majesty's service."—*Globe.*

SIR JAMES ALEXANDER'S ACADIE;

OR, SEVEN YEARS' EXPLORATION IN CANADA, &c.

2 vols., post 8vo, with numerous Illustrations, 12s. bound.

"Replete with valuable information on Canada for the English settler, the English soldier, and the English Government; with various charms of adventure and description for the desultory reader."—*Morning Chronicle.*

"No other writer on Canada can compare with the gallant author of the present volumes in the variety and interest of his narrative."—*John Bull.*

STORY OF THE PENINSULAR WAR.

A COMPANION VOLUME TO MR. GLEIG'S "STORY OF THE BATTLE OF WATERLOO."

With six Portraits and Map, 5s. bound.

"Every page of this work is fraught with undying interest. We needed such a book as this; one that could give to the rising generation of soldiers a clear notion of the events which led to the expulsion of the French from the Peninsular."—*United Service Gazette.*

LADY LISTER KAYE'S BRITISH HOMES

AND FOREIGN WANDERINGS.

2 vols., post 8vo, 10s. bound.

"Unrivalled as these volumes are, considered as portfolios of aristocratic sketches, they are not less interesting on account of the romantic history with which the sketches are interwoven."—*John Bull.*

THE NEMESIS IN CHINA;

COMPRISING A COMPLETE

HISTORY OF THE WAR IN THAT COUNTRY;

From Notes of Captain W. H. HALL, R.N.

1 vol., Plates, 6s. bound.

"Capt. Hall's narrative of the services of the *Nemesis* is full of interest, and will, we are sure, be valuable hereafter, as affording most curious materials for the history of steam navigation."—*Quarterly Review.*

"A work which will take its place beside that of Captain Cook."—*Weekly Chronicle.*

ADVENTURES OF A LADY DURING HER TRAVELS IN AFRICA.

2 vols., 10s.

POETICAL WORKS OF BARRY CORNWALL,

Cheaper Edition, 6s.

ZOOLOGICAL RECREATIONS.

By W. J. BRODERIP, Esq., F.R.S.

Cheaper Edition, 1 vol., post 8vo, 6s. bound.

"We believe we do not exaggerate in saying that, since the publication of White's 'Natural History of Selborne,' and of the 'Introduction to Entomology,' by Kirby and Spence, no work in our language is better calculated than the 'Zoological Recreations' to fulfil the avowed aim of its author—to furnish a hand-book which may cherish or awaken a love for natural history."—*Quarterly Review.*

THE WANDERER IN ITALY, SWITZERLAND,

FRANCE, AND SPAIN.

By T. ADOLPHUS TROLLOPE, Esq. 1 vol., 6s. bound.

ADVENTURES OF A GREEK LADY,

The Adopted Daughter of the late Queen Caroline.

WRITTEN BY HERSERF,

2 volumes, post 8vo, price 12s. bound.

POPULAR WORKS OF FICTION.

MERKLAND. By the Author of "Margaret Maitland." 3 v., 31s. 6d.

PASSAGES IN THE LIFE OF MRS. MARGARET MAITLAND, OF SUNNYSIDE. Written by Herself. New and Cheaper Edition. 1 v., 10s. 6d.

MR. WARBURTON'S REGINALD HASTINGS. Third and Cheaper Edition. 1 v., 10s. 6d.

NATHALIE. By Julia Kavanagh, Author of "Woman in France," 3 v., 15s.

FALKLAND. By Sir E. Bulwer Lytton. 1 v., 5s.

VIOLET; or, THE DANSEUSE. 2 v., 10s.

ANNE DYSART; or, THE SCOTCH MINISTER'S DAUGHTER. 3 v., 15s.

1771846R0020

Printed in Great Britain
by Amazon.co.uk, Ltd.,
Marston Gate.